WAY TO
PLAY BRIDGE

ea

THE RIGHT WAY TO PLAY BRIDGE

The Complete Reference to Successful Acol Bidding and the Key Principles of Play for Improving Players

Paul Mendelson

RIGHT WAY

Constable & Robinson Ltd
3 The Lanchesters
162 Fulham Palace Road
London W6 9ER
www.right-way.co.uk
www.constablerobinson.com

First published in the UK 1994

This new completely revised and updated edition published
by Right Way, an imprint of Constable & Robinson, 2008.

A copy of the British Library Cataloguing in Publication
Data is available from the British Library

ISBN: 978-0-7160-2196-4

Printed and bound in the EU

1 3 5 7 9 10 8 6 4 2

DEDICATION

To my parents
who have always come up trumps

ACKNOWLEDGEMENTS

I rather stumbled into bridge while at school and, had it not been for my friends, I would certainly not have continued to be fascinated by the game.

Elizabeth Hallifax, an experienced teacher, was the only member of my club who would play with me when I was a teenager. Now we teach a class together each week, and it is a delight.

Roland and Suzanne Saillard were my first students, and their support, enthusiasm, and achievement after all this time are a source of considerable pride.

Space precludes me from naming everyone but I must mention a few more bridge friends. Pat Cotter, British International and distinguished columnist, who has always emphasized the value of the partnership, and Norman Fried and Peter Hardyment – my two regular partners – the former with whom it is always a pleasure to play and laugh and eat vast Chinese dinners, and the latter to whom I owe much of my advanced knowledge. This comes as a result of his relentless experiments which have a tendency to drive me, the opponents, and anyone eavesdropping, quite crazy...

CONTENTS

QUICK REFERENCE INDEX

This index can take you immediately to a bidding chart which summarizes its preceding text, making this book ideal as an at-the-table guide. Use them to check your bidding, and to build up partnership understanding. Do *not* use them to criticize your partner, still less your opponents.

INTRODUCTION

To enjoy this book you will want to know what bridge is about. Perhaps you have been playing the game for years, or maybe you've just graduated from a year of beginners' classes and want to know more.

This book assumes that you know what a Weak No-Trump is, that you have heard of Stayman and Blackwood, and that you have some idea how to play the cards. If you don't, then try *Bridge for Complete Beginners*, another of my books.

If you think this sounds about right for you, or frankly even if you think it sounds too basic, then you are probably holding the one book which can both enhance your enjoyment of the game, and increase your ability to win. *The Right Way to Play Bridge* is designed to streamline your bidding and focus your play by demonstrating the excellence of modern Acol bidding, and the logical thought processes behind some of the key plays. There are no complicated gadgets and, whilst bridge is a partnership game, there is plenty of scope for improvement as an individual.

The pleasure to be derived from outwitting your opponents and pleasing your partner is well worth some gentle reading.

Not only that, *The Right Way to Play Bridge* is the ideal companion for your afternoon or evening game (or, come to that, your morning one as well). If you are lost for a bid, you can use the Quick Reference Index to take you to the right bidding charts. Whenever you sense you might have been more successful, you can find the relevant section in a moment.

And so you have an authoritative, clear and ever-patient teacher at your side.

The beauty of any language is that it evolves. It does so sometimes through necessity, but often simply for convenience. Abbreviations become more widespread, common phrases packed with background meanings appear more regularly, and slang passes into the vocabulary of even the most refined speakers.

So it is with bridge. We are limited to a confined vocabulary and so there is always the battle to streamline the language. Following a major survey by Eric Crowhurst – one of our leading theorists and experts – which took in players of all standards, and from my study of the experts' idea of Acol, I am able to demonstrate in this book an Acol bidding language that is almost 100 per cent logical. This makes it simpler to learn and easier to remember.

In the Key Principles of Card Play chapter, you can examine clear examples which demonstrate the vital thoughts required whenever you are not dummy. (Dummy may have vital thoughts as well, but often they have nothing to do with bridge...) These processes are straightforward, but their application will reap huge benefits.

Although this book deals exclusively with a Weak NT (showing 12–14pts), much of it is relevant for the dedicated Strong NT (15–18pts) player too. However, I must tell those players that the Weak NT occurs far more frequently, is more accurate, more pre-emptive, and far more logical. With this book to guide you, I urge you to repent and convert...

As for those who claim to be "intuitive" players, or who just fancy a gamble, bridge offers plenty of scope to demonstrate your famed sixth sense – but peculiarly, it seems to improve the more you do. Opportunities galore exist to outwit the opposition with bluff and bombast – although it helps if *you*, at least, know what's really going on. In other words, learn the skills first, and then you'll recognize the right moment to be "clever".

Finally, I have had to face the age-old problem of how to refer to your partner in all my examples. I've opted for "he" and "him". Those with their finger on the pulse of political correctness might have wished me to utilize a unisexual term, but it strikes me that repeating the word "partner" several hundred times is too high a price to pay...

Paul Mendelson
London

1

EVALUATING YOUR HAND

This chapter deals with the way you value the thirteen cards in your hand. It deals with that initial moment of pleasure, or pain, as you pick up your cards, and later after you have heard your partner bid. Your hand's value also changes when your opponents bid, and this is dealt with further on in the book at various stages, in particular see COMPETITIVE BIDDING, page 89.

You should read this first chapter now, even though it may contain ideas with which you are not yet familiar and then, as you read the rest of the book, you may care to return here.

Strange as it may seem, the worth of a hand of bridge is changing all the time. Because its value alters as the bidding progresses around the table, it is essential that you are aware of those changes, and the effect they should have on your bidding.

Opening the Bidding
If you are the first player to make a positive bid, you should count your High Card Points (HCP), and extra points for long suits. You should add 1pt for every card over four in any suit.

Hence, with this hand:

♠ AKJ87   You have 12 HCP, and you may add a further
♥ 6   point for both the fifth spade, and the fifth
♦ KJ987   diamond, making your total 14pts. On this basis,
♣ 84   the hand certainly warrants an opening bid. 1S is
          correct.

You should not add any points for your shortages as, until
your partner bids, you will have no idea whether those shortages will be useful or not.

There are several types of opening bid which rely partly or
wholly on distribution. See Acol Light Opener, page 16, and
Pre-emptive Bidding, page 65.

The basic requirement of opening the bidding is 12 HCP.
You can open with fewer points
only with a 6-card suit or longer.

Responding to an Opening Bid
Above all, you are hoping that you and your partner have a *fit*:
i.e. at least 8 cards in the same suit, between your two hands.
This 8-card fit ensures that, if you select it as your trump suit,
your side will hold the clear majority of trumps and thus that
tricks will be that much easier to win.

For this reason, the moment you know that you have an 8-
card fit in partner's suit (whether this is on your first response,
or at a later stage in the auction), you should add extra points
for shortages as well as length in your other suit(s). This is the
scale:

Doubleton   add 1pt
Singleton   add 3pts
Void   add 5pts.

Once you know that you have a fit with partner, these shortages in other suits in your hand will be useful, because partner

will be able to trump losing cards in these suits with your trumps.

If your partner bids a suit in which you are *short*, this heralds the bad news that you and your partner may have a misfit – a hand where you do not hold 8 cards in any one suit between your two hands. On hands where your side has no fit, tricks will be much harder to come by, and you should ensure that the bidding does not reach too high a level.

Therefore, the basic thinking is:

> *If your partner bids a suit in which you hold a shortage,*
> *this makes your hand worse.*
> *If partner bids a suit in which you hold 3 cards or more,*
> *your hand improves.*

If you cannot support your partner's suit, you should continue to count only HCP and extra points for length in a suit (or suits). Later in the auction, if it becomes clear that you <u>do</u> have an 8-card fit with partner, then you may add points for shortages.

Having Been Supported by Partner
If you opened and you now have confirmation that you have a fit with partner, you too may add extra points for shortages, <u>provided that these shortages are not in suits your partner has previously bid</u>.

This is the scale:

Doubleton   add 1pt
Singleton   add 2pts
Void   add 3pts

The reason that these values are lower than those for the hand which initially supports a suit is that you often only want to trump cards in one hand, leaving length in the other, with which to draw out the opponents' trumps. Therefore, shortages in the hand which first bids the suit are not worth quite so much.

The Shape of the Hand

By now, you should be able to value your hand in terms of points. This is half of your hand evaluation complete. The other half concerns the shape of your hand, and the way you describe this to your partner.

"Modern Acol, with a Weak No-Trump" is the system to which this book adheres. This makes the shape of the hand a vital consideration.

Having assessed point-strength, it is vital to establish in your own mind whether your hand is balanced or distributional.

Your hand is balanced if the number of cards in your two longest suits adds up to eight or less.

The only exception to this rule concerns hands with a 4-4-4-1 shape. There are no more than eight cards between the two longest suits but, because this shape contains a singleton, the hand cannot be deemed to be balanced. I make my own suggestions for coping with these awkward hands later in the book (see page 45). You will not be alone, should you find them difficult. The only consolation I can offer is that, the world over, in social games and world championships alike, the 4-4-4-1 shape causes bridge players to have nightmares.

The key to bidding balanced hands is remembering that, as the opener, an opening bid or a re-bid of No-Trumps guarantees a balanced distribution. Hence:

With a balanced hand you must either open the bidding with 1NT or 2NT, or, open with a suit and then re-bid No-Trumps.

As the opener, failure to bid No-Trumps within the first two rounds of bidding would deny a balanced hand.

Incidentally, your hand does not change shape just because your partner bids a suit in which you are short. In other words, your partner cannot "fill the gap" – suddenly making your hand balanced – when he bids a suit in which you hold a singleton.

As you will see in forthcoming chapters, later in the auction you may decide that a NT contract is your partnership's best spot, but the first two rounds of bidding must be reserved for accurate description of your hand.

All other hands are distributional and you will see how to deal with them from page 14.

Partnership Targets
The following chart gives you an idea of your target contract, as a partnership, with various combined point counts.

Sometimes, you will know exactly your partner's point count from his bidding. At other times, you may have to assume a certain point count before making a judgement as to the level to which it is safe to take your partnership.

Whilst this chart is quite accurate for NT contracts, it is only a rough guide for suit contracts, as the power of an 8-card fit (and of length and shortages in other suits) is much harder to gauge. Note that these point counts *include* your distributional points for length and shortages, as summarized in the chart on page 7.

PARTNERSHIP TARGETS

Pack contains a total of 40 HCP

Combined partnership point count	Target Level	Number of tricks
20–22	1-level	7
23–24	2-level	8
25–26	3-level	9
26–28	4-level	10
29–32	5-level	11
33–35	6-level	12
36+	7-level	13

These are <u>minimum</u> point counts for each level. Some point counts overlap to cover both NT and suit contracts.

Part score = 21–24pts
Game = 25–32pts
Small Slam = 33–35pts
Grand Slam = 36pts+

DISTRIBUTIONAL POINTS

Until a fit (8 cards or more in the same suit) has been found, only points for <u>length</u> should be added to your HCP total.

Add 1pt for each card over four in any suit in your hand.

Only once you know that you have an 8-card fit, or better, can you add points for <u>shortages</u>.

When supporting partner's suit:

doubleton	add 1pt
singleton	add 3pts
void	add 5pts.

Having been supported by partner, only add points if your partner has not previously bid the suit(s) in which you hold shortage:

doubleton	add 1pt
singleton	add 2pts
void	add 3pts.

If you have no fit (a misfit) with partner's hand, ensure that the bidding does not reach too high a level. If necessary, deliberately bid to one level lower, on your combined point count, than the chart on the previous page recommends.

2

OPENING THE BIDDING

Balanced Hands – Opening 1NT

If your hand is balanced and contains 12–14 points, you <u>must</u> open the bidding with 1NT. This opening bid describes your hand in one go, removes the need to find a re-bid, and puts the ball firmly in partner's court. Knowing what you have, he will either decide the final contract immediately, or ask you about a specific element of your hand.

Having opening 1NT, you have limited your hand, and you never make another free bid. Only if partner's response asks you to describe your hand further should you ever bid again.

Should you open 1NT if your hand contains a 5-card minor suit? Yes. If your hand is balanced, the minor suit is of far less importance than telling partner your shape and point count all in one easy bid.

Your targets on every hand of bridge run as follows:

1st An 8-card fit (or better) in a major suit.
2nd A NT contract.
3rd A minor suit contract.

A major suit and a NT contract are almost as good as one another. The major-suit fit gets top billing because it is often safer, especially if it is a 4-4 fit. Opening 1NT allows you to reach NT contracts with ease. The use of Stayman (see page 22) removes any fear of missing a 4-4 fit in a major suit.

Minor suit contracts should be avoided because of their feeble scoring value, and should only be considered when both major suit and NT contracts are impossible.

So, what about hands containing 12–14pts and a 5-card major suit? Should they be opened with 1NT?

Experts are divided on this question. Many believe that a 5-card major suit should take priority over a 1NT opening, whilst some feel that the balanced nature of the hand should be expressed immediately.

I recommend compromise:

(a)	♠ 97532	(b)	♠ AKJ75
	♥ KQ3		♥ 64
	♦ QJ6		♦ 963
	♣ AJ		♣ AJ8

(a) With 13 HCP, the choice is between opening 1NT, or opening 1S, and then re-bidding 2S. With the quality of the suit as poor as this, and with an even distribution of high cards, 1NT seems the better description of the hand.

(b) The major suit is good quality – well worth bidding and re-bidding. There are also two unguarded suits. 1S is the superior opening now.

You should open a 5-card major suit in preference to 1NT, unless the quality of the suit is so poor that you judge 1NT to be a better description of the hand.

This rule works well for everyday use. If you are building a regular partnership, or you play with the same group, you may wish to experiment by always opening the 5-card major regardless, before forming your own conclusions.

This type of decision is greeted with approval by partners when you make the right choice, and derided when the result is not as might be hoped. Look out for the people who change their view after looking at the result, rather than thinking about the problem. These characters form the group known as "result-merchants". They will have you believe that they are terribly good players because they always know what everybody should have bid and every card they should have played. Unfortunately, this "wisdom" is only apparent after the hand is over...

Balanced Hands with more than 14pts
With these hands you need to consider your re-bid before deciding on your opening bid. With more than 14pts you are too strong to open 1NT, so you should open a suit, and plan to re-bid NTs. Obviously, if you hold a 5-card suit, you should open the bidding with this.

> *With two (or three) 4-card suits, always open 1H;*
> *never open 1S.*
> *If you do not have four hearts,*
> *open either minor suit (see below).*

This ensures that you open the bidding with a low-ranking suit, allowing your partner to show his 4-card major suit if he holds one. However, it is better to open 1H than 1C or 1D since, as a major suit, this must be your priority. To open 1S, however, would force partner to show a suit at the 2-level.

> *With two 4-card minor suits, generally open the weaker quality*
> *one as this may inhibit a dangerous lead from your opponent.*

♠ A84   If you open the bidding here with 1C, your partner
♥ AQ   may reply 1H and you will rebid 1NT (15–16pts).
♦ 5432   However, your opponent may well lead a diamond,
♣ KQJ9   which will not please you. If you open the bidding
           with 1D and end up in No-Trumps, your opponent
           will probably not lead a diamond, and this gives
           you an advantage.

Since you will try not to play in a minor suit, the only way that
you will end up having your weak suit as trumps is if your
partner supports you (with four cards) and there is no chance
of a No-Trump contract. In that case, you still hold an 8-card
fit and should succeed.

Only if partner supports a major suit, or responds a major
suit in which you hold 4-card support, would you not make
your intended NT re-bid.

*Provided that you hold the requisite point count, always ignore
a minor suit fit in favour of making your NT re-bid.*

In the following examples you need to decide your opening
bid, and prepare for your re-bid – although you cannot be
certain of it until you have heard partner's response. For more
details on the re-bid consult Chapter 5, OPENER'S RE-BID.
   Partner's hands are shown alongside:

(a)

♠ AJ76	♠ 985	Note that you re-bid 1NT rather than
♥ J5	♥ A86	1S. As your hand is balanced, you
♦ K96	♦ AQ543	must mention NTs within the first two
♣ AK52	♣ Q3	rounds of bidding. Had you re-bid
		1S, this would have promised more
1C	1D	than eight cards between your two
1NT	3NT	suits – at least five clubs and four
		spades.

(b)

♠ AQ43	♠ KJ76
♥ KJ76	♥ Q52
♦ Q3	♦ 94
♣ AJ6	♣ KQ82
1H	1S
3S	4S

You open 1H; partner replies 1S. Rather than making your intended 2NT rebid, you should support partner's major suit. The 8-card major suit fit − usually the safest contract − is reached with ease. Note that the responder's chief priority is always to show a major suit at the 1-level.

(c)

♠ AQ	♠ 652
♥ KJ8	♥ Q43
♦ Q963	♦ AK742
♣ AQ43	♣ J6
1C	1D
2NT	3NT

Here, partner responds with a <u>minor</u> suit in which you hold support. You should ignore this in favour of your planned NT re-bid. This results in the best Game contract being reached.

So, the one and only time you do not make your planned NT re-bid with a balanced hand is when partner responds a 4-card major suit for which you have 4-card support.

1C – 1H – <u>1NT</u>
The 1NT re-bid in this sequence shows 15–16pts. This is sound, because partner's 1-level response promises a minimum of 6pts, and this opposite 15–16 gives a total of 21–22: just right for 1NT.

If responder holds more points, he can raise the level.

If the bidding runs 1D – 2C, partner's change of suit at the 2-level is now promising a minimum of 8pts. Your lowest available re-bid of 2NT still shows only 15–16pts. This too is sound, as you now have a combined minimum of 23–24pts − suitable for 2NT.

Note that this is completely different from 1D – 2D, in which partner's response is weak, indicating maybe just 6pts.

OPENING WITH BALANCED HANDS

12–14pts	Open 1NT.
15–16pts	Open a suit; Re-bid NTs at lowest available level.
17–18pts	Open a suit; Re-bid NTs jumping a level
19–20pts	Open a suit; Re-bid 3NT. *In each of above, with 4-card support for a* *response of a major, support this in favour of* *making your NT re-bid.*
20–22pts	Open 2NT. *See 2NT Opening and Responses to 2NT,* *page 74.*
23+ pts	Open 2C; Re-bid NTs at appropriate level. *See 2C Opening and Responses to 2C, page 75.*

For that you must hold a full 17–18pts to re-bid 2NT (to bring you up to the 23–24pts you require). With fewer, you should just pass.

Distributional Hands – Suit Opening Bids

A hand is distributional if it contains nine cards or more
between its two longest suits.

When assessing the strength of this sort of hand before there has been any bidding at the table, you should count only High Card Points (HCP) but pay attention to the length of suits in your hand. The general rule is that you may add on an extra point for every additional card over four in each suit.

You should not count points for shortages (listed on page 7) yet. The reason for this is that shortages are only of use once you have established a trump fit, and you know that partner is not about to bid the suit in which you are short. If your partner does bid a suit in which you are short, this makes your hand worse, because it is the beginning of a misfit.

You require 12 HCP to open the bidding, except when your hand contains a 6-card suit or longer. At this stage, you need to keep in mind what you will rebid too since, if you open the bidding with a suit and your partner changes the suit, you must bid again.

Always start at the 1-level unless your hand can make at least 8 tricks on its own. (For stronger openings, see page 73.)

On hands with more than one suit, the underlying rule about which suit to bid first is always:

Length before strength – always open your longest suit.

And on hands when you hold two suits of equal length:

With two 4-card suits, always open 1H;
without hearts, open a minor suit.
With two 5- or 6-card suits, open the higher ranking suit
except if they are clubs and spades when,
for reasons of bidding space, it is better to open 1C.

With two 4-card suits being your longest, your hand would be balanced – 8 cards or fewer between the two longest suits. If you held over 14pts you would open the bidding with the appropriate suit, planning to re-bid NTs. Therefore, it is logical to say that:

If you open one suit, and then re-bid another suit,
you are promising at least five cards in the first suit
and four cards in the second.

In other words, you possess at least nine cards between the two suits (5+4).

This fundamental difference between balanced and distributional hands is the crux of modern Acol bidding.

Distributional Hands – Acol Light Opener

The Acol light opening simply takes into account the strength of a long suit. It is made on hands of 10 or 11 High Card Points with a high quality 6-card suit. There is nothing special about this bid; it just reflects the fact that often the playing strength of such a hand is greater than one with 13 or 14 HCP.

For example, contrast these two hands:

(a)	♠ KQJ987	(b)	♠ KJ432
	♥ 8		♥ AK4
	♦ AJ62		♦ K432
	♣ 42		♣ 7

Both hands warrant an opening bid of 1S. The so-called "light opener" in (a) is more likely to produce tricks than the stronger hand (b).

Hand (a) contains at least six tricks if the hand is played in spades, whereas (b) will provide four or five at most.

The key to the Acol light opener then, is a good quality 6-card suit.

3

RESPONDING TO 1NT

As Chapter 2 makes clear, once your partner has opened 1NT, he has described his hand pretty fully. As responder, it will be for you to decide what the final contract should be. Sometimes, you will be able to leap directly to the right spot, whilst on other occasions you will take the opportunity to ask partner to describe his hand further.

As always, your priorities will be an 8-card major suit fit, followed by a NT contract. Only if both of these are impossible should you settle for a minor suit contract.

Limit Raises
Holding a balanced hand, it is a matter of arithmetic. You require a minimum of 25pts for 3NT. Add your point count to partner's known minimum (in this case 12) and bid to the *limit* of your combined hands.

If there is no chance of 25pts between you, pass. If you hold enough for 2NT if partner has the minimum, bid 2NT, and partner can raise to 3NT if he actually holds 14pts. With enough for 3NT even if partner has only the minimum, bid 3NT straightaway.

That is the thinking. Converted into points, you need to remember in response to partner's 1NT opening, that if you hold:

0–10pts	NB
11/12pts	2NT } *but with a 4-card major(s)*,
13–18pts	3NT } *use Stayman (see page 22)*.
19pts+	Consider a Quantitative Raise (see page 137).

Over 2NT, partner then passes if he has minimum points, and bids 3NT if maximum. With 13pts, he will need to hold a 5-card suit, or good intermediates (10s and 9s) to bid 3NT. Failing this, he should pass, and settle for a part score.

Weak Take-Out
Sometimes partner opens 1NT, and you are faced with a very poor hand, including a long suit.

Because you are WEAK you should TAKE your partner OUT of 1NT into the comparative safety of a trump contract.

In response to 1NT, 2D, 2H and 2S are Weak Take-Out bids, promising 0–9pts and at least a 5-card suit. (Note: 2C is not a Weak Take-Out bid, as it is reserved for the "Stayman" convention but, should you hold a long club suit, it is still possible to make a Weak Take-Out through the convention. See page 27.)

You are not expecting to make the contract after a Weak Take-Out, you just believe that it will be less awful than leaving partner to suffer in 1NT.

Because this is a damage-limitation manoeuvre, it is vital to remember that:

> *After a Weak Take-Out bid of 2D, 2H or 2S,*
> *the 1NT opener <u>never</u> bids again.*

(a)   ♠ J96432   (b)   ♠ KJ874
     ♥ –   ♥ 64
     ♦ 7532   ♦ A643
     ♣ 432   ♣ J5

(a) If you were to pass 1NT, your hand would be useless to partner, and 1NT would fail by many tricks. Bid 2S.

Partner will always pass, recognizing this as a Weak Take-Out. In spades, your hand will provide at least three trump tricks, perhaps four. Instead of partner going down four or five tricks in 1NT, you will probably fail by only one or two in 2S. Not a success, but definitely less of a disaster!

(b) 1NT may well make on this hand, but you should still bid 2S.

With two doubletons, the hand is more likely to play well with a 5-card trump suit than in NTs.

Game-going Hands

These are responder's distributional hands containing 12pts or more. Basically, the Acol system says that an opening hand opposite an opening hand should result in Game.

This leaves a nasty problem on hands containing 10 or 11pts – too strong for a Weak Take-Out, and probably too weak for a Game force.

In general, when such hands contain only 4- or 5-card suits, it is best to be cautious and make an underbid – a bid which makes partner think you hold a weaker hand than you actually have. However, 6- and 7-card suits can be upgraded (think of them respectively as being worth an extra 2 or 3pts) to allow you to push on for a Game contract.

If you do not make a Weak Take-Out, then you are heading for Game as all jump bids opposite 1NT inevitably lead to a Game contract.

For the purposes of responding to 1NT, hands containing long minor suits with 10pts or more should be counted as balanced ones, most sensibly played in NTs. You scarcely ever respond by showing a minor suit.

(a) ♠ KJ6   (b) ♠ 6
     ♥ Q3   ♥ J7
     ♦ J6   ♦ AKQJ852
     ♣ AQ9873   ♣ 874

On both (a) and (b) you should raise partner's 1NT to 3NT without hesitation. Both hands are worth Game, but 11 tricks in 5C or 5D are unlikely to roll in on either hand.

On hand (b) do not worry about the lack of stoppers in the majors and the club suit. As partner holds no points in diamonds, he is likely to hold good cards in the other three suits.

Of course 3NT may fail, but it will undoubtedly be your best chance of scoring a Game contract.

With a long minor suit and modest, but sufficient, points, always support NTs rather than bidding the suit.

STRONG HANDS WITH MINOR SUITS
In the Acol system, a bid of 3C or 3D shows a hand with slam interest. It is unconditionally forcing to Game, and likely to contain wild distribution, with a large number of points. Suppose you hold:

♠ 6   Here, you might respond 3D and, if partner
♥ 4   fails to support you, you could then head for
♦ AQJ753   a club contract. If partner holds even one Ace
♣ AKQ42   and K♦, 12 tricks in 6C or 6D are likely to be
             stacked up in front of you pretty quickly.

As you might imagine, these sorts of hands do not crop up all that often. Indeed, I cannot remember the last time I saw a 3C or 3D response correctly applied. Most importantly, you should remember that 3C and 3D are invitations to a slam, and that with Game-going hands 3NT is nearly always the correct spot.

STRONG HANDS WITH MAJOR SUITS
With a good major suit and a Game-going hand, your target is to play in that suit at the Game level, or higher. Hands contain-

ing 6-card major suits or longer are easy to express. As partner has opened 1NT, his hand must contain at least two cards in the major suit, so you know that you hold the vital 8-card fit between you. So, on Game-going hands:

With a 6-card major suit, or longer, jump straight to 4H or 4S.

When your hand contains a 5-card major suit, your first target is still to discover whether you hold an 8-card fit in that suit.

With a 5-card major suit, bid 3H or 3S. This forces partner to bid 3NT if he holds only a doubleton in this suit, or to bid 4H or 4S if he has 3-card support or longer.

Whatever the 1NT opener holds in the major, and whether he holds minimum or maximum points, the sequence must result in a Game contract.

In response to 1NT, you hold:

(a) ♠ K98532   (b) ♠ KJ7
    ♥ AQ3   ♥ KQ953
    ♦ A42   ♦ A65
    ♣ 4   ♣ 84

(a) Respond 4S. You have enough points for Game (25 or more), and you hold a 6-card suit. Your partner must hold at least a doubleton spade, so you know that you hold an 8-card fit between you.

(b) Respond 3H. You could bid 3NT, but a major suit fit is top of your priorities. Your response informs partner that you want to be in Game, that you hold a 5-card heart suit, and that he should decide which Game to play in. With three or more hearts, he will raise you to 4H; holding only a doubleton, he will bid 3NT.

*With two 5-card major suits, you should first bid 3S,
and, if partner fails to support that suit, by calling 3NT,
you can then bid 4H.*

Partner must have 3-card support for one of your suits, as he
would not have opened 1NT with two doubletons. As always,
you respond the higher ranking of two 5-card suits first, allowing you to return to the lower one should you not receive
support.

Even if your Game-going hand only contains one 4-card
major, you may still have an 8-card fit in the suit. However:

*You never bid a suit in response to 1NT
unless it contains at least five cards.*

You use the "Stayman" convention to discover if the 4-4 fit
you need exists.

Stayman

"Stayman" is a conventional bid – to be agreed by the partnership before play (although almost everyone plays it) – and
is used mainly in response to an opening bid of 1NT or 2NT.
It is designed to locate a 4-4 fit in the major suits and – with
one exception I shall come to on page 27 – consequently:

*You will only use Stayman when your hand contains
at least one <u>four</u>-card major.*

It may be used on both balanced and distributional hands
and, subject to distribution, can be used on any point count.
Most of the time however, it is Game-going manoeuvre.

A response of 2C opposite 1NT (or 3C opposite 2NT) asks
partner if he holds a 4-card major suit. Partner's responses
are extremely simple:

2S shows a 4-card spade suit.   } The 3-level responses to
2H shows a 4-card heart suit.   } 2NT have the same
2D denies a 4-card major suit.   } meanings.

Should he hold both major suits, it is usual to respond 2H (or 3H over 2NT) first, and later show the spade suit if necessary. If he happens to hold a poor 5-card major suit, he should treat it as a 4-card suit.

As with all bidding, you should be prepared for an answer which does not please you, as well as one which does. Imagine that you hold the hand below, and incorrectly use the Stayman Convention:

♠ KJ87   Your partner opens 1NT, and you bid 2C. Partner
♥ Q752   responds 2D, denying a 4-card major. What can
♦ J86   you bid now? Bidding 2H or 2S might result in a
♣ J2   disastrous contract, and bidding 2NT would
            promise 11 or 12 pts.

The fact is that the hand above is unsuitable for Stayman because, although it contains both major suits, there is nowhere to go if partner does not hold either of them.

For this reason:

With balanced hands containing 4-card majors you need 11pts or more to use Stayman, allowing you to return to 2NT (with 11 or 12pts) or 3NT (with 13pts or more) if partner does not hold the major suit you hoped for.

There are other types of hand on which to use Stayman, which you will see in a moment. Most importantly, remember:

Having used Stayman, if partner does not respond what you hoped, you should next bid whatever you would have done had you not used Stayman in the first place.

For example, with the following hands you bid 2C opposite 1NT, and each time partner responds 2D:

(a) ♠ KJ86   (b) ♠ QJ98
    ♥ Q742   ♥ A7
    ♦ AJ8   ♦ A65
    ♣ K8   ♣ 7532

(a) You could have responded 3NT in the first place. Correctly, you checked for a 4-4 fit in either of the major suits, but having discovered that none exists, you now bid 3NT as intended.

(b) 2NT would have been your response had you not known about Stayman. Now that there is no 4-4 fit in spades, you should return to 2NT. If partner had maximum points for his 1NT bid, he will raise you to 3NT.

It is not all bad news. Once again, partner has opened 1NT, you responded 2C but this time partner replies 2H:

(c) ♠ KJ87   (d) ♠ 72
    ♥ Q97   ♥ KQ87
    ♦ AK74   ♦ KQJ6
    ♣ J6   ♣ J32

(c) Your partner has responded the major suit in which you are not interested, so you return to 3NT.

Note that you have shown a 4-card spade suit by this action. Why? In order to use Stayman you must have a 4-card major in your hand. It is obviously not hearts, as you would have supported your partner, so it must be a 4-card spade suit.

Therefore, if your partner actually holds both majors, he can now safely bid 4S, knowing that a 4-4 fit exists.

You see, everybody has to be awake at the table!

(d) You have found a 4-4 fit. Raise partner to 3H. This shows 11 or 12 HCP. He can then pass with a minimum hand, or bid 4H with a maximum one. Had your hand contained 13pts or more, you could have jumped straight to 4H yourself.

(e)
West	East
♠ Q753	♠ AK82
♥ KQ65	♥ A43
♦ AJ4	♦ K876
♣ Q4	♣ 87

1NT	2C
2H	3NT
4S	

(e) When West shows a 4-card heart suit in response to Stayman, it is of no interest to East, who now bids 3NT to show a balanced hand containing 13pts or more.

However, as East must hold one 4-card major in order to use Stayman – and it is obviously not hearts – West can convert this Game contract to 4S, as he now knows a 4-4 spade fit exists.

There are also hands when partner's response to Stayman disappoints you, for which you will have sensible re-bids other than NTs. These Weak Take-Out style bids do not require any minimum point count. For example:

(f)
(f)	(g)
♠ K654	♠ 9876
♥ Q6532	♥ 7654
♦ 3	♦ 95432
♣ 853	♣ –

(f) It is quite safe to use Stayman here. Bid 2C, and if partner responds 2H or 2S, you can pass, having found the best Weak Take-Out spot. If partner bids 2D, you can return to 2H, which is what you would have bid had you not used Stayman in the first place. As this is a response at the 2-level it is still a Weak Take-Out bid, and partner should always pass.

(g) With this hand, it is even more necessary to take rescue action. Once again, Stayman offers you the best chance of finding the least awful contract. Whatever partner bids – including 2D – you will pass. Partner will probably gulp when you pass 2D, but when he sees your hand he will realize how imaginative you have been.

So the real rule about the number of points you require for Stayman is this:

You can use Stayman with any number of points, provided you have a sensible re-bid whatever your partner responds.

This is still quite consistent with the need for a minimum of 11pts with balanced hands, as with them your cheapest re-bid can only be 2NT, requiring 11 or 12pts.

This also means that it is quite permissible to use Stayman even on this type of hand:

Your partner opens 1NT:

♠ KJ75
♥ –
♦ AKJ8654
♣ 83

Your priority is an 8-card fit in a major, so you bid 2C looking for a 4-4 spade fit. If partner responds 2S, raise him to 4S. If he bids 2D or 2H, jump to 5D. In other words, you have tried for a major suit fit, but when this has failed, you have settled for a minor suit.

The only time that you will use Stayman without a 4-card major in your hand is when you are planning to make a Weak Take-Out in clubs. In order to do this, you need to bid 2C. Your partner will respond believing this to be Stayman; you then re-bid 3C. This tells partner that you intended to make a Weak Take-Out in clubs.

Note that, despite your weak hand, you have managed to contract yourself at the 3-level, so there had better be a pretty good reason for taking partner out of 1NT:

(h) ♠ Q3   (i) ♠ 5
      ♥ J85   ♥ 4
      ♦ J72   ♦ 8532
      ♣ KJ742   ♣ QJ98765

(h) Pass. You have no reason to take partner out of 1NT, and certainly not to the 3-level. 1NT may well make, 3C will have no chance.

(i) Here, 1NT has no chance whatsoever, and 3C may not go that badly, especially if partner has some high cards in diamonds. Bid 2C (Stayman), then 3C over whatever partner responds.

> *Do not think about making a Weak Take-Out in clubs*
> *unless you are certain that 1NT will be a disaster.*
> *To do so, you will probably hold at least a 6-card club suit.*

Also, do not confuse 2C then 3C, with bidding 3C immediately, which is a slam try in clubs – there is quite a difference...

RESPONDING TO 1NT

NB	Balanced hand.	0–10pts
2C	Stayman. *Your hand must contain at least one 4-card major, and a sensible re-bid, unless you are planning a Weak Take-Out in clubs.*	0+pts
2D, 2H, 2S	Weak Take-Out. 5+ card suit.	0–9pts
2NT	Balanced hand. *Opener passes with minimum, raises to 3NT with maximum.*	11/12pts
3C, 3D	Slam interest. 5+ card suit. *Very distributional hand.*	16+pts
3H, 3S	5-card suit. Forcing to Game. *Partner bids 4H/S with 3+ card support, or 3NT with a doubleton.*	12+pts
3NT	Balanced hand. *May contain long minor suit, with fewer HCP.*	13–18pts
4H, 4S	6+ card suit	12+pts
4NT	Quantitative (not Blackwood). *Partner passes if minimum, bids 6NT if maximum. (See Page 137.)*	19/20pts
5NT	Quantitative. *Partner bids 6NT if minimum, bids 7NT is maximum. (See page 138.)*	23/24pts
6NT	To play – partner always passes. *(See page 6.)*	21/22pts

4

RESPONDING TO A SUIT OPENING

With fewer than 6pts your general rule must be pass. Otherwise there are four main actions you can take in response to a suit opening by partner:

1. Change the Suit
A change of suit at the 1-level promises a minimum of 6pts, and a 4-card suit. There is no upper limit to the number of points you may hold, or the number of cards in the suit you bid. Therefore it is vital that your partner remembers that he <u>must</u> re-bid once you have changed the suit. That is to say, a change of suit is forcing for one round.

A change of suit at the 2-level promises a minimum of 8pts, and a 4-card suit, except for 1S – 2H, which promises a 5-card heart suit. This exception is to cope with the fact that 1S – 2H has catapulted the bidding up to a high level after only two bids, and therefore your bid needs to contain extra information to make it worthwhile – namely, the 5-card suit. Again, there is no upper limit on points or suit length, and partner must bid again.

2. Support Partner's Suit

These responses promise 4-card support for partner's suit. They are known as "Limit Raises" because you are bidding to the limit of your combined hands assuming partner holds a minimum hand. This makes it easy for him: if he does hold a minimum, he just passes your bid; if he holds more he continues bidding.

The point counts are the same for all four suits, for example:

$$1H - 2H = 6{-}9\text{pts} \qquad 1H - 3H = 10{-}12\text{pts}$$

1H – 4H or 1S – 4S shows a weak hand (fewer than 10 HCP) but one with excellent support for partner's suit, and useful distribution.

Including distributional points (see page 7), your total here should come to 13pts+.

Occasionally, holding a weak hand, you may have to make a simple raise (for example 1H – 2H) with only 3-card support. This should be reserved for hands where no better alternative exists.

(a)   ♠ K973   (b)   ♠ K97
      ♥ 6   ♥ 6
      ♦ Q732   ♦ 86543
      ♣ J432   ♣ J542

On both (a) and (b) you should raise your partner's opening bid of 1S to 2S. Partner will expect you to hold 4-card support as in (a), but on hand (b) a simple raise to 2S is quite acceptable. You are not strong enough to change the suit at the 2-level (8pts+) and a response of 1NT is unsuitable with your singleton heart. In any case, following the rule on page 11, you will only VERY rarely open 1S on a 4-card suit and so it is highly likely that you and your partner will hold an 8-card fit in spades. Additionally, because you hold a singleton heart, even a 4-3 spade fit would play nicely, as your partner can trump losing hearts in your hand with your 3-card trump support.

With a weak hand (6–8pts), in response to partner's 1H or 1S opening bid, prefer to support him with 3-card support, rather than bidding 1NT.

When you hold 4-card support for a major-suit opening, and 13–15 HCP, you must make a bid which shows your opening hand and 4-card support. In the old days, a "Delayed Game Raise" might have been used but now a "Pudding Raise" is recommended. This is because:

With 4-card support for partner's major suit, you must support him immediately.

In response to a 1C, 1D, 1H or 1S opening bid, a Pudding Raise is an immediate jump to 3NT. You would never waste bidding space like that if you suspected that you might want to play in 3NT; you would change the suit and await partner's re-bid before making that decision.

The Pudding Raise shows:
• 4-card support for partner's suit

• 13–15 points

• no singleton or void (if you have a shortage, you might use a "Splinter Bid").

To avoid confusion with a new partner, check that he knows the meaning of this bid. For example, your partner opens 1S and you hold:

♠ KJ87
♥ A52
♦ Q54
♣ A95

With 14pts, you are too strong to raise to 3S, so you must make a Pudding Raise. You respond 3NT and, if your partner's hand contains any shortages at all, he will convert to 4S or look for a slam. If his hand happens to be completely balanced, he may choose to pass your 3NT response.

Although it may seem odd to pass 3NT when you have a 4-4 fit in a major suit, on the very rare occasions when this occurs, it will probably be for the best. After all, if you can't do any trumping in either hand, why have a trump suit?

Opposite a minor suit opening bid, the Pudding Raise would deny that the responder held a 4-card heart or spade suit, since to show a major suit is responder's top priority. It is more likely that the opener will pass the 3NT Pudding Raise response since, even with a minor suit fit, 3NT is the preferred spot.

With 16pts+, consider a Jump Shift as in 4. below.

3. NT Responses

In the same way that when you support your partner's suit you do so to the limit (with a Limit Raise), balanced hand responses of No-trumps involve bidding to the full extent of your combined hands on the assumption that partner holds a minimum opening bid. Hence, they define your hand and are known as "Limit Bids".

On page 34 you will find the complete range of these NT responses. Beware though, because 1NT may also be used for a different reason – to keep the bidding open on hands of 6–9pts. This is explained in a moment.

Before responding with a NT bid, you must remember your greater priority and responsibility, namely that:

Responder must always first show at the 1-level
a 4-card major suit of any quality.

With four hearts or spades in your hand, you <u>must</u> first respond 1H or 1S, rather than making your NT response. The NT Limit Bid can always be made later. (See RESPONDER'S SECOND BID, page 53.)

In consequence, a response of NTs to a suit opening denies a 4-card major, or support for partner's major. There is one exception to all this, which is when you hold a 4-card heart suit, and your partner opens 1S. This is because in Acol, as has been explained in **1**. above, 1S – 2H would show a 5-card heart suit. Therefore, you just have to remember that after an opening of 1S, a NT response may include a 4-card heart suit.

There is no real danger of missing a 4-4 fit in hearts though, because, if partner opened "length before strength", but has four hearts he is bound to re-bid in them. (Note that if he was 4-4 in spades and hearts, he should have opened 1H.)

As NTs are of far greater worth than a minor suit, it is possible that you will hold 4-card support for partner in clubs or diamonds and still choose to respond NTs.

Do remember that a jump to 2NT or 3NT is very wasteful of bidding space – hoicking the level up very quickly before you have heard partner's re-bid. Therefore these NT responses should only be used when you are certain that they best describe your hand.

Finally, whilst 2NT and 3NT responses definitely show a balanced hand, the response of 1NT may not show a completely balanced hand. It is sometimes really used just to keep the bidding open in case opener holds an absolute maximum hand for his 1-level opening.

For example, after an opening bid of 1S, all these hands qualify for a 1NT response:

(a)	♠ 2	(b)	♠ 43	(c)	♠ 54
	♥ Q853		♥ KJ6		♥ AJ4
	♦ K532		♦ J76432		♦ 5432
	♣ Q542		♣ J7		♣ Q832

Even though (a) and (b) are not balanced hands, any other response would exaggerate your slender values – a change of suit to the 2-level would promise at least 8pts. 1NT keeps the bidding alive, without over-exciting partner.

4. Jump Shift

This involves a change of suit, jumping a level of the bidding. It is a slam-going procedure unconditionally forcing to Game. Only use it when you believe you are in the slam zone and, most importantly, you know which suit is going to be trumps. (See Chapter 10, SLAM BIDDING.)

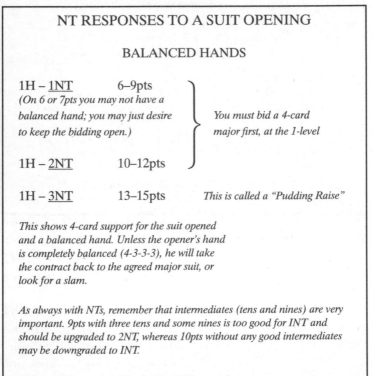

NT RESPONSES TO A SUIT OPENING

BALANCED HANDS

1H – <u>1NT</u>   6–9pts
(On 6 or 7pts you may not have a
balanced hand; you may just desire   *You must bid a 4-card*
to keep the bidding open.)   *major first, at the 1-level*

1H – <u>2NT</u>   10–12pts

1H – <u>3NT</u>   13–15pts   *This is called a "Pudding Raise"*

This shows 4-card support for the suit opened
and a balanced hand. Unless the opener's hand
is completely balanced (4-3-3-3), he will take
the contract back to the agreed major suit, or
look for a slam.

As always with NTs, remember that intermediates (tens and nines) are very
important. 9pts with three tens and some nines is too good for 1NT and
should be upgraded to 2NT, whereas 10pts without any good intermediates
may be downgraded to 1NT.

1H – <u>4NT</u>   Blackwood Convention
          asking for Aces – see page 132.

RESPONSES TO SUIT OPENINGS

PASS 0–5pts   *Any distribution.*

CHANGE OF SUIT

At 1-level 6pts+	*4-card suit or longer.*	} *Opener*
At 2-level 8pts+	*4-card suit except for 1S – 2H,*	} *must*
	which needs 5-card suit.	} *re-bid.*

NT RESPONSES

1NT	6–9pts	}	*No 4-card major suit*
2NT	10–12 pts	}	*except possibly opposite 1S opening.*

3NT 13–15pts   *Pudding Raise – showing 4-card*
                   support for opener's suit with a balanced hand.

RAISING OPENER'S SUIT

1H – 2H	6–9pts	*4-card support; rarely 3-card support with outside shortage.*
1H – 3H	10–12pts	*Always 4-card support, or longer.*
1H – 4H	fewer than 10pts	*Excellent support and distribution.*

With 16pts+ consider a Jump Shift – see page 129.

Remember that NT responses to 1C, 1D, or 1H all categorically deny a 4-card major, regardless of quality. Over 1S, a NT response may contain a 4-card heart suit, as 1S – 2H promises a 5-card suit.

A 2NT response shows a balanced shape, whilst a 1NT response may not be balanced, as it may be used merely as a "noise" with which to keep the bidding open for one round.

A 4NT response would be Blackwood, asking for Aces, and not one designed to show point count. This sequence is most unlikely, as with a hand considering a slam you would not waste all that bidding space by leaping to 4NT immediately. That would prevent partner from giving you further information with his re-bid.

However, it has been known...

5

OPENER'S RE-BID

When opening the bidding with a suit you guarantee that, should your partner change the suit, you will have a <u>re-bid</u> ready. This is essential, as partner's response may be made on any hand from 6pts upwards, and the bidding cannot be allowed to die.

Balanced Hands
With a balanced hand you will have opened a suit because you have too many points to have opened 1NT. Unless you have located a fit in a major suit, your re-bid will now be NTs.

1D – 1S   1S – 2D
<u>1NT</u>   shows 15–16pts   as does   <u>2NT</u>

1D – 1S   1S – 2D
<u>2NT</u>   shows 17–18pts   as does   <u>3NT</u>
                                    This re-bid may also be made
                                    with 19 or a poor 20pts.

1D – 1S
<u>3NT</u>   shows 19 or a poor 20pts

These re-bids are all based around the principle of limit bidding. If you open 1D and partner responds 1S, he is promising a minimum of 6pts. Based on that minimum, you will need 15–16pts opposite partner's 6pts in order to make 1NT (about 21–22pts), and so that is what your re-bid shows.

Hence, when partner responds at the 2-level, promising a minimum of 8pts, your re-bid of 2NT will still show only 15–16pts, as partner's minimum of 8pts opposite your 15–16 should be enough for 2NT (about 23–24pts).

For the opening bid and the re-bid, describing your hand accurately is vital. Remember that, as pointed out in Chapter 1, your hand does not change shape mid-way through the auction. Either your hand is balanced or it isn't.

Later, when you and your partner have both bid twice, description may take second place to decision. After all, the level of the biding is rising, and one of you will have to make a decision on the contract.

(a) ♠ Q   (b) ♠ QJ84
     ♥ J42   ♥ J3
     ♦ AJ742   ♦ KQ6
     ♣ AQ42   ♣ AK74

(a) You open the bidding with 1D, preparing to re-bid 2C. If partner happens to bid 1S this should not distract you from continuing the description of your hand. The hand is not balanced – you have nine cards between your two longest suits – and so you must not mention NTs within the first two rounds of bidding. That would guarantee a balanced hand, misleading partner.

     Later, a NT contract may be the best option but it is far too early to decide the final contract now. For the first two rounds, your duty is to describe your shape and point count to partner.

(b) You open 1C, planning to re-bid 1NT. When partner responds 1D, you should not be distracted from your intentions by worrying about holding no high cards in hearts. All you will be telling your partner by re-bidding 1NT is that you hold a balanced hand with 15–16pts. Also, do not be tempted to re-bid 1S. Your failure to re-bid NTs would deny holding a balanced hand, and promise partner more than eight cards between the two suits you have bid. He would be justified in assuming you hold 5 clubs and 4 spades.

Limit Raises in Partner's Suit
Whether your hand is distributional or balanced, if partner responds with a major suit, and you hold 4 cards in that suit, it is your duty to support him immediately.

With balanced hands, this takes precedence over re-bidding NTs to show a point count. (If partner responds with a minor suit, you should re-bid NTs as planned.)

As the title suggests, you *raise* your partner's suit to the *limit* of your combined hands, on the assumption that partner has responded with minimum points. Therefore, the more you bid, the stronger you are. For example, you hold:

♠ KQ76   You open 1C – the lower-ranking of your two 4-
♥ A4   card suits, planning to re-bid NTs. Partner responds
♦ J73   1S. Now, you should reject the NT re-bid in favour
♣ AJ53   of supporting partner's major suit. Remembering
that an 8-card trump fit always produces extra tricks, and assuming that partner has shown a minimum of 6 HCP for his response, you should raise him as follows:

with 12–15pts make a simple raise, i.e. raise to 2S.
with 16–18pts make a jump raise, i.e. raise to 3S.

with 19–20pts   jump to Game – even if partner has only
                 minimum points, you should be in with a good
                 chance of making the contract.

When you open 1S and partner responds 2H, you have lost one
level of the above bidding with which to describe your hand.
However, because your partner has responded at the 2-level, he
promises a minimum of 8pts, and a 5-card heart suit (see page
29). So in this instance, the re-bids run as follows:

1S – 2H
<u>3H</u>   a simple raise, now shows 12–16pts.

1S – 2H
<u>4H</u>   a jump raise, now shows 17–20pts.

Distributional Hands

With these hands, there is a variety of re-bids available,
depending on the strength and shape of your hand. The
expressions "single-suited", "two-suited", etc, refer to hands
which are dominated by a single suit, or two suits, etc.

I SINGLE-SUITED HANDS

You open the bidding with 1S, and partner responds 2C:

(a)	♠ KQJ54	(b)	♠ KQ8763	(c)	♠ KQJ1098
	♥ A64		♥ A7		♥ 6
	♦ K62		♦ AQ6		♦ AK
	♣ 43		♣ J4		♣ Q764

(a) Re-bid 2S, showing a 5-card suit. You have a fairly
    minimum opener, and the spade suit is the only feature
    worth emphasizing.

(b) Re-bid 3S. With a 6-card suit, and more points than partner might expect from an opening bid, you should jump re-bid.

(c) Re-bid 4S. With a self-supporting trump suit (a suit that requires no support from partner whatsoever), and a good fit with partner's suit, Game is almost certain, even if partner has minimum points.

II TWO-SUITED HANDS

You open the bidding with 1S, and partner responds 2C:

(a) ♠ KQJ54   (b) ♠ KQ763   (c) ♠ AKQ98
    ♥ A642   ♥ A72   ♥ 6
    ♦ K6   ♦ 6   ♦ AK432
    ♣ 43   ♣ QJ43   ♣ Q7

(a) Re-bid 2H. Bidding two different suits guarantees at least 5-4 distribution. As responder can still return to your first suit at the 2-level, the re-bid shows no extra values. If your re-bid forces the responder to the 3-level in order to return to your first suit, then you have "reversed", a manoeuvre which promises extra values. (See next page.)

(b) Re-bid 3C. As the 2C response may only be a 4-card suit, you must have 4-card support yourself. Once again you are showing 5-4 distribution. With 16/17pts or more, you would jump to 4C to show extra strength. Partner could then continue if he has more than minimum points.

(c) Rebid 3D. Because your partner's response has only promised 8pts, this jump-rebid in a new suit shows a minimum of 17pts, usually more, and is <u>forcing to Game</u>. Your minimum distribution should now be at least 5-5 in your two suits, but could be even more shapely (i.e. 6-5 or 6-6).

III THREE-SUITED HANDS

These are most often the dreaded 4-4-4-1 shape, which is so difficult to bid. (See 4-4-4-1 Hands – page 45.)

However, sometimes 5-4-3-1 hands should be treated differently from the usual re-bids and Limit Raises.

For example, you open 1H, and partner responds 1S:

(a) ♠ 7   (b) ♠ KJ7
     ♥ AK753   ♥ AK753
     ♦ Q742   ♦ Q742
     ♣ A54   ♣ 5

(a) You re-bid 2D as planned to show your 5-4 distribution.

(b) Your planned re-bid was 2D, but on this occasion it is better to re-bid 2S. If partner is weak, you do not want to miss the chance of playing in spades at the 2-level. If he is strong the bidding will continue anyway. The keys are your singleton club, and that you are supporting a major suit.

The Reverse
"Reverse" is really a misnomer but it is the way everyone describes these two bids. It refers to an opening bid and re-bid taken together.

There are two ways of defining a reverse:

(a) If the opener bids a new suit at the 2-level, which is higher in rank than the one with which he opened

or

(b) An opening bid and then a re-bid which would force partner to go to the 3-level in order to give preference back to the first suit.

These definitions amount to exactly the same thing, but are slightly different ways of identifying the sequence.

Examples:

(a) 1H – 2C (b) 1D – 1S (c) 1S – 2D (d) 1C – 1H
    2S – 3H   2H – 3D   2H – 2S   1S – 2C

(a) A reverse. Opener has re-bid a suit at the 2-level which is higher in rank than his first suit. In order to return to opener's first suit, responder has had to bid at the 3-level.

(b) Again, a reverse, for the reasons above.

(c) Not a reverse; responder can give preference at the 2-level.

(d) Again, not a reverse. Opener has re-bid a higher ranking suit, but at the 1-level, allowing partner to give preference at the 2-level.

Hopefully you can now identify when partner has reversed – or when you have for that matter. But what is the significance of a reverse?

Take example (a) above. Responder bids 2C opposite an opening bid of 1H. This response promises a minimum of 8pts. Opener now re-bids 2S, asking responder to choose between the suits. If responder wishes to give preference to hearts he will have to do so at the 3-level.

Now, if opener only holds 12 HCP and responder only 8pts, they will find themselves at the 3-level with only 20pts between them, and almost no chance of making their contract. Therefore:

In order to reverse, opener's hand must contain at least 16pts, and always more cards in the first suit than the second.

This then means that responder need not be afraid of giving preference at such a high level.

Indeed, because these reverse sequences show 16pts or more, they are <u>forcing</u> for one round. This means that responder <u>must</u> dredge up one more bid, even if he has only minimum points.

At the table, it is often easy to overlook a reverse. At all times:

> *Translate what all the bidding means so far,*
> *before deciding what you will bid next.*

If you do that, you will spot reverses.

So what are you to do when you hold a weak hand, but in order to make your guaranteed re-bid, you would be reversing?

For example:

♠ KQ86   You open 1H; partner responds 2C. You must not
♥ AQ643 re-bid 2S as this would be a reverse promising at
♦ Q43   least 16pts. Instead, just re-bid 2H. There is no
♣ 8   chance of missing a 4-4 fit in spades, because if
responder holds four spades he knows that it is his responsibility to show them. If he has not done so already, he either does not have four spades, or he will be bidding them on the next round.

> *With hands of 12–15pts, you must not reverse.*
> *To avoid doing so, just re-bid your first suit,*
> *rather than showing the second suit.*

Finally, it is worth mentioning to the more "imaginative" amongst you, that it is not sensible (still less, desirable) to manufacture a reverse, by bidding your suits in the incorrect order. Some players do this because they want to produce a forcing sequence. Deliberately bidding suits in the wrong order has only one effect. It gets you into the wrong contract.

Either the distribution and points for a reverse exist, or they do not.

For responses to the reverse – see page 61.

4-4-4-1 Hands

This shape of hand causes everybody problems, especially the opener – most especially when having to find a re-bid – as it is the one shape that is neither balanced (it contains a singleton) nor distributional (no more than 8 cards between two suits).

There are many theories about how to treat these hands. In modern Acol, the easiest method is to open the usual 4-card suit. Hearts if possible; otherwise a minor suit.

What you do next is somewhat ignored. If partner bids one of your 4-card suits, then life is easy, but if he bids your singleton as is likely, then whatever you re-bid will be a lie, because:

(a) You cannot re-bid your own suit unless it contains five cards.

(b) You cannot re-bid a second suit without promising 5-4 distribution.

(c) You cannot re-bid NTs, because you do not hold a balanced hand.

To avoid the worst repercussions of such misleading information, I recommend the following action:

With 4-4-4-1 hands of 12 and 13pts, just pass.

If partner opens, you will be well placed to respond and, if the opponents open your singleton suit, you will be holding a perfect Take-Out Double (see page 106).

With 14pts or more, open hearts if you have four of them, or open a minor suit. Never start with 1S.

If partner responds with your singleton suit, re-bid NTs at the appropriate level. Your 14pts will have to suffice for the cheapest NT re-bid.

This still involves misinforming your partner, but you will end up in more NT contracts and fewer 4-3 fits and, whilst you will not make every contract that results, there is generally less scope for disasters.

If you are playing with a regular partner, it is worth discussing how to treat this shape of hand. If not, you can afford to experiment, but remember that all systems have their good and bad days. If you play with the sort of partner who sifts through your hand after a throw-in, you may have a bit of explaining to do when 13pts hit the table…

Come to think of it, you shouldn't be playing with a partner like this. He obviously doesn't trust you and wishes he could bid your hand as well as his own. Don't bother playing with him again…

Trial Bids
These are gadgets within the Acol system, which alter some of the underlying principles. It is advisable to discuss with any new partner whether you will be playing these.

There are two distinctive types of Trial Bid which should be included in your basic system:

I TRIAL BID AFTER MAJOR SUIT AGREEMENT

This bid occurs only after the sequence 1H – 2H or 1S – 2S.

The opener, holding a hand on which he considers Game a possibility, re-bids a suit in which he requires help, usually one containing three quick losers.

If responder is able to reduce the number of losers in this suit, either because of a high-card holding or through shortage, he raises opener to Game in the agreed suit.

If he is unable to assist in that suit, he signs off at the 3-level in the agreed suit, and a poor Game contract is avoided.

Let's take a look at a couple of examples which illustrate the accuracy of the sequence:

	West	*East*		*West*	*East*
(a)	♠ AKQ87	♠ 9643	(b)	♠ 963	♠ J742
	♥ K7	♥ A542		♥ AKQ98	♥ J742
	♦ 742	♦ 8		♦ 63	♦ KQ5
	♣ AJ9	♣ Q653		♣ AK5	♣ Q6

(a) West opens 1S and is raised to 2S by East.

Game is a possibility but West is worried about his three quick losers in diamonds. West should now re-bid 3D, asking East if he can reduce the number of losers in that suit. East, holding a singleton diamond, now knows that his distribution is just where partner requires it, and jumps to 4S.

(b) West opens 1H; East raises to 2H.

West now makes a Trial Bid of 2S, showing a weak suit, and asking partner if he can help to reduce the likely three losers. East's spade holding cannot offer any help, and therefore he signs off by bidding 3H. West now passes dutifully, and an unmakable 4H is avoided.

Notice that in (a) Game is reached when responder holds a minimum, but in (b) Game is unmakable even though he holds a maximum for his simple raise. Again, this reinforces the value of complementary shape, rather than simply adding together points.

The Trial Bid accurately assesses whether the hands are really fitting, or whether the good points in each hand are in the same suit – what the experts call "duplication of values". It is almost more satisfying to stay out of a bad contract which you feel everyone else would have fallen into, than to reach a good one on slender values. Managing either, or better still both, will improve your scores in the long run.

Basically then, the Trial Bid shows a suit with three quick losers, and asks if partner can help in that suit.

Imagining the sequence: 1H – 2H
                           3C – ?

Partner's responses are as follows. With:

Three losers in the club suit, return to 3H, signing off.

Two losers in the club suit –
  having raised with a minimum hand (6–7pts), re-bid 3H.
  having raised with a maximum hand (8–9pts), jump to 4H.

One or *no* losers in the club suit, jump to 4H.

Having made the Trial Bid, you then pass partner's response.

Once you are clear on the use of the Trial Bid, it is acceptable to play around with it a little. For example, on this hand:

♠ AKJ72   After the sequence 1S – 2S, you might bid 3D –
♥ AKQ76   not as a try for Game, but to seek a possible slam.
♦ J43   If partner leaps to 4S in response, this may be
♣ –   based on a singleton diamond in his hand, and a
          slim 6S might just be making. It will be a gamble,
          but a clever use of the Trial Bid has enabled you
          to unearth the possibility.

II MINOR SUIT TRIAL BIDS

I prefer to call these bids "Stopper-Showing Bids for No-Trumps" because they are used to show stoppers in different suits when looking for a 3NT contract. However, some players still call them "Minor-Suit Trial Bids".

These bids can be used after the sequences 1C – 2C or 1D – 2D and 1C – 3C and 1D – 3D.

Because the opener is unlikely to want to play in 5C or 5D, when his partner supports him, he may wish to investigate for a 3NT contract. Unlike the Major Suit Trial Bids, these bids show where you hold <u>good</u> cards – or stoppers – seeking a No-Trump contract. Holdings such as: Ax, Kx, Q10x, Jxxx are all considered stoppers for No-Trumps.

If you hold no stoppers in the outside suits, just return to your agreed suit at the lowest available level.

To use a Stopper-Showing Bid for No-Trumps, you must believe that you could hold sufficient points for Game.

After the sequence 1D – 2D, the opener would require 17pts+ to look for Game.

After the sequence 1D – 3D, opener would need 14pts+ to look for Game.

	West	East		West	East
(a)	♠ 87	♠ AJ9	(b)	♠ AK4	♠ QJ2
	♥ AK7	♥ 52		♥ 83	♥ 42
	♦ AK742	♦ Q853		♦ K43	♦ AQ86
	♣ A96	♣ J532		♣ AKQ54	♣ 7632

(a) West opens 1D; East raises to 2D.

West re-bids 2H, showing a stopper in the suit. East co-operates by bidding 2S, showing a stopper in that suit. Happy that all the suits are covered, West now re-bids 2NT showing the usual 17/18pts. East, having supported opener's suit with close to a maximum raise, can bid 3NT, which is laydown.

(b) West opens 1C; East raises to 2C.

West now re-bids 2D, showing a stopper in the suit. East re-bids 2S, showing a stopper in that suit, but denying a stopper in hearts as, if he had held one, he would have bid 2H first, being the cheaper bid.

West now knows that neither partner has hearts covered.

He jumps to 4C to show a very strong hand and to suggest 5C as a final contract. East, holding a maximum for his raise to 2C, co-operates by bidding 5C, which is an excellent Game contract.

(c) *West*   *East*

♠ 32	♠ A64
♠ KJ4	♥ 865
♦ AKJ5	♦ Q43
♣ AJ62	♣ KQ73

1C	3C
3D	3S
3NT	

West opens 1C and East raises to 3C. West now bids 3D as a Stopper-Showing Bid for No-Trumps and East replies with 3S. This denies a heart stopper, since he should bid his stoppers in ascending order. Now that West knows that he has all the suits covered, he can bid 3NT with some confidence.

Some more experienced players adopt these stopper-showing bids whenever there has been a minor suit agreement in the auction, even when it is not the first two bids. For example:

(d) *West*   *East*

♠ AK542	♠ 63
♠ A3	♥ 852
♦ 52	♦ K8
♣ A854	♣ KQJ932

1S	2C
3C	3D
3H	3NT

West opens 1S and East responds 2C. West raises to 3C. East now bids 3D, showing a stopper there and West replies 3H, also indicating a stopper. East now bids 3NT, which is a much easier contract than 5C.

You may feel that East's bid of 3D was very brave but, with a long minor suit, you should always be seeking to play in 3NT rather than five of a minor and you can often survive with just a single stopper in a side-suit.

If you feel happy with this sequence, then you and your partner should agree to play that, after a minor suit agreement at the 2- or 3-level, any new suit will be stopper-showing, seeking a No-Trump contract. That is the way all experts play and if you adopt these methods you will reach many more 3NT contracts. Not all will make, but you will find that you are far more successful than you were, trying to play in 5C or 5D, or guessing whether to play in 3NT or not.

PLEASE TURN OVER FOR TRIAL BID CHART

TRIAL BIDS

(To be made as a try for a Game contract)

After a major suit agreement   1H – 2H or 1S – 2S:
A re-bid in any other suit by opener says:
"I am interested in bidding Game, but I am worried about three quick losers in this suit."

Responder re-bids as follows:

With 3 losers also in the suit		3 of agreed suit.
With 2 losers	and a minimum raise	3 of agreed suit.
	and a maximum raise	Game in agreed suit.
With 0 or 1 loser in the suit		Game in agreed suit.

Opener should pass whatever responder re-bids.

After a minor suit agreement, the Trial Bid – or Stopper-Showing Bid for No-trumps – shows in which suit you hold a stopper and asks partner to bid the suit where he holds a stopper.
Both you and your partner will bid where you have stoppers in the cheapest (ascending) order.
If he holds no stopper in an unbid suit, he returns to the agreed minor suit.
If he holds a stopper in the one unbid suit, or in both unbid suits, he bids no-trumps himself.

To use a Minor Suit Trial Bid, you must be interested in Game.
After a simple raise (1C – 2C), you require 17pts or more to start using Trial Bids.
After a jump raise (1C – 3C), you require 14pts or more to start using Trial Bids.

6

RESPONDER'S SECOND BID

Development of the Auction

(You have responded to partner's opening bid, and he has now made a re-bid. You must now find your own re-bid, which may include No-bid.)

Showing Preference

When partner opens with one suit, and re-bids a second suit, you are required to steer the partnership into the best – or maybe least awful – contract available, even if you are holding minimum points in relation to your initial response.

Take this hand for example:

♠ AQJ98	♠ 76	Partner, on the left, opens with 1S;
♥ QJ43	♥ 95	you respond 1NT, to keep the bidding
♦ A74	♦ K863	alive, and he re-bids 2H. Tempting
♣ 5	♣ K6432	as it is to pass quickly as you are so

weak, you must remember that partner has shown you at least five spades and four hearts. Therefore, it is essential that you adjust the contract from 2H (where you only have six trumps between you) to 2S, where at least you jointly hold the majority of trumps. Neither contract will be a great success, but 2S will be better.

Sometimes Showing Preference seems to make matters worse:

♠ AJ753   Partner opens 1D and you, holding this hand,
♥ 876   respond 1S. Partner re-bids 2H and, once again,
♦ 876   you may be tempted to pass. Here, however,
♣ Q4   partner has reversed (see page 42), promising
more diamonds than hearts. Even though you have to bid up to a higher level, 3D, it will be correct to do so, placing your partner in an 8-card fit, rather than a 7-card fit. In any case, the reverse is forcing, so you have to bid something.

Lastly, you sometimes have to return to partner's first suit, even though you personally prefer the other suit. For this reason it has been given the misnomer "false preference". This is misleading because it refers only to what you hold in your own hand. Good bidding hasn't only to do with your thirteen cards. It must involve at least your partner's hand as well and, better still, all four hands.

♠ Q5   Partner opens 1S; you respond 2D, he re-bids 2H.
♥ Q53   Although you prefer hearts, you should return to
♦ AJ643   2S, because your partner is showing at least 5-4 in
♣ 842   his spades and hearts, and a 5-2 trump fit is superior to a 4-3 fit. This is because the length in trumps in partner's hand will be better able to cope with any bad breaks in the suit which may arise.

There is also the possibility that partner has 6-4 in spades and hearts, and is quite correctly checking for a possible heart fit. He will not be pleased to be playing in a 4-3 heart fit if a 6-2 spade fit is available. And if opener is 5-5 in hearts and spades, in all probability he will be bidding on, and you will be able to show your superior support for hearts later.

So, the rule for Showing Preference is this:

Always return partner to his first suit, unless you hold two more cards in his second suit than in his first.

This two added cards concept hearkens back to the key principle that length in trumps is far more important than strength.

The opener, too, must remember the vital element of receiving preference, which is often much weaker than receiving support.

Preference is often given on only a doubleton, sometimes less, and NEVER promises any extra points.
It is merely an adjustment of the contract.

Pass, or bid on?
Thankfully, you are not always under so much pressure when holding a weak hand in the responder's re-bid position.

If partner re-bids NTs, or supports your suit, he is making a Limit Bid. If you hold minimum points, you just pass; if you have more, you can raise your partner accordingly. As always, translate what the bidding means before choosing your next bid.

Responding to a minimum level re-bid of partner's suit usually needs distinct discipline.

Partner opens 1H, you respond 1S, and partner re-bids 2H. This bidding suggests that he holds a 5- or 6-card heart suit, and about 12–15pts. What should you bid next on these hands?

(a)	♠ KJ87	(b)	♠ KJ753	(c)	♠ KJ98
	♥ Q32		♥ 5		♥ 7
	♦ J632		♦ KJ743		♦ KJ64
	♣ J6		♣ 43		♣ Q432

(a) Pass. You are very happy for partner to play in hearts, however, if his maximum is 15pts, there can be no chance of Game.

(b) Pass. You are not happy with hearts as trumps, however, if you bid again, you will be promising enough points to make Game a possibility, and with only 8pts and a misfit, that is not the case. In order to show your second suit, you would have to re-bid at the 3-level, taking the bidding way beyond a safe level.

(c) Pass. Some might try 2NT. Almost always this will be a disaster, because a misfit is never any good for NTs – where is your source of tricks?

After a minimum level re-bid by opener in his original suit, pass on all hands of fewer than 11pts, unless you hold excellent trump support and useful distribution. Above all, when there is a misfit, keep the bidding low. Never try to rescue partner by re-bidding NTs.

Game-going Hands
With more than the minimum shown by your initial response – usually hands of at least 10pts – you must bid something other than that which merely Shows Preference (which is always weak). Thankfully, you have a whole range of stronger actions available:

I SUPPORT PARTNER (Jump preference)

♠ K75   Partner opens 1S; you respond 2D; he re-bids 2H.
♥ A4   Now that you know he holds at least five spades,
♦ KJ754   you can support them. Do not bid 2S. That would
♣ 964   just be Showing Preference – jump to 3S, which
            shows genuine support, and invites partner to re-
bid Game if he holds more than minimum points. With 13pts or more, you should bid to Game yourself.

II RE-BID YOUR SUIT

♠ KQJ743   Partner opens 1H; you respond 1S; he re-bids
♥ 8   2D. A re-bid of your suit now suggests a 6-card
♦ Q76   suit as, with only five cards, you should give pref-
♣ Q98   erence (or jump preference) to one of partner's
           two suits. This 2S re-bid is not forcing, but it is
constructive; if partner holds more than a minimum with even
doubleton support for you he will continue bidding. With
more than 11 HCP, you should jump to 3S, or make a 100 per
cent forcing bid, such as Fourth Suit Forcing, see below.

III BID NTs

The NT responses are exactly the same on the second round
as they were on the first, with one important exception. For
responder to jump to 3NT on the second or third round of
bidding is not a "Pudding Raise". It is a natural bid which,
unless opener has made a reverse, shows 13–15pts.

However, if you and your partner bid three suits, and you
then bid NTs, you are promising TWO stoppers in the un-bid
suit. Without them, you must consider Showing Preference or
giving support to one of partner's suits, or, using "Fourth Suit
Forcing".

IV BID THE FOURTH SUIT

Part of the Acol System is the understanding that a bid of the
fourth suit is played as Fourth Suit Forcing. As the name
suggests, this bid _forces_ partner to continue describing his
hand. It also _denies_ _two_ stoppers in the fourth suit as, if you
held them, you would have bid NTs, as above.

Fourth Suit Forcing (4SF)
Your partner opens 1H; you respond 1S, and partner re-bids
2C. Holding each of these hands, what are your next moves?

(a) ♠ KJ98   (b) ♠ Q9843   (c) ♠ KJ98
     ♥ Q2   ♥ K2   ♥ Q3
     ♦ AK43   ♦ A43   ♦ J32
     ♣ 542   ♣ A54   ♣ AJ85

(a) 3NT. You have two stoppers in the un-bid suit – diamonds – and 13pts. Only if partner is very distributional will he bid on.

(b) 2D. Fourth Suit Forcing. The bid tells partner that you do not have two stoppers in diamonds – or you would have now bid NTs, as above – but you do hold a good hand with Game ambitions and you wish to hear partner describe his hand further. Re-bidding spades or NTs would be wrong.

(c) 2D. Fourth Suit Forcing again. You could support partner's clubs but, by forcing partner to bid again, you leave open the possibilities of playing in NTs, if he holds stoppers in diamonds, or of playing in hearts or spades. It's a long way to 5C…

4SF can be used whenever you wish to force partner to bid again. Although a NT contract is often the ambition of the 4SF bidder, other contracts may well result after making this bid.

To use Fourth Suit Forcing, you require enough points to cope with whatever response partner might make to the 4SF bid. Usually 11pts is considered the minimum at the 1- or 2-level, and enough points for Game for use at the 3-level.

You do not promise any minimum length in the fourth suit. You might hold a singleton, or you may have a 5-card suit.

At the 1- and 2-levels, you do not require any high cards in the suit whatsoever – your bid is just a general enquiry.

At the 3-level, partner *will expect* you to have *one* stopper in the suit. This will allow him to bid NTs happily, when he holds just one stopper in the fourth suit opposite you.

You open 1H, partner responds 1S, you re-bid 2C, and he then uses 4SF, 2D. You have been asked to describe your hand further:

What will you bid, holding these hands?

(a)	♠ 87	(b)	♠ 65	(c)	♠ 7	(d)	♠ K76
	♥ AJ986		♥ AQJ86		♥ AK9753		♥ AJ986
	♦ AQ		♦ 8		♦ A4		♦ 8
	♣ Q984		♣ AK652		♣ QJ87		♣ AKJ4

(a) 2NT. You have shown your shape correctly earlier. Now you can tell partner about the two diamond stoppers, and suggest a NT contract. Bid straight to 3NT when you hold 14pts or more, as partner's use of 4SF has promised at least 11pts.

(b) 3C. Having promised 5-4 in hearts and clubs, this re-bid of your second suit is the correct way to show the 5-5 distribution.

(c) 3H. The jump re-bid enables you to show a 6-card suit.

(d) 3S. This shows 3-card support, and a better than minimum hand. With weaker hands of this shape, you would have to re-bid 2S rather than 2C initially.

If the opener has already imparted all the information he can about his hand, he should simply re-bid his 5-card suit at the lowest available.

How the sequence develops from this point will obviously be up to the responder who will, after all, have heard you describe your hand three times. Most good players assume that, once Fourth Suit Forcing has been adopted, the bidding sequence is now Game forcing. That is to say that neither the opener nor the responder can pass any bid short of a Game

contract. However, there may be rare occasions when the 4SF
bidder himself, having discovered what further information
he can from his partner, decides that – despite holding values
for Game – there is no fit and therefore a likelihood that
Game may not make. For that reason, the 4SF bidder only
may, rarely, pass before Game is achieved.

What do you do next if you hold a hand like this, and the
bidding runs as follows?

Partner opens 1H; you respond 1S; and he re-bids 2C:

♠ AJ864   Your first instinct may be to bid 2D anyway, but
♥ 7   partner will take that as 4SF, and assume that you
♦ AQJ87   hold poor diamonds. You have two alternatives:
♣ Q4   (1) you could jump to 3D which would show your
               strong natural suit. However, playing the final
contract in diamonds is unlikely to be a success, whereas a NT
contract may get home courtesy of your good diamonds and
enough High Card Points. (2) You could bid 3NT, which would
be correct, promising two stoppers in diamonds, and denying
support for partner's major suit.

There are many further uses of Fourth Suit Forcing which
require partnership agreement and understanding. This is
another area well worth discussing with your regular partner
or group of players.

Finally, it is worth mentioning that a bid of a new suit at the
3-level is always 100 per cent forcing.

If you know that Game is your target, but you are not yet
sure of the denomination in which it should be played, you
can be assured that your partner will continue bidding by
using either 4SF, or by introducing a new suit at the 3-level.

Responding After a Reverse

I WITH WEAK HANDS

Because partner has reversed, you know that his hand contains at least 16pts. Your bid from now on will be based on that knowledge.

With a weak hand, you should choose one of these courses of action:

Partner opened with 1D, you responded 1S, and he re-bid 2H:

(a)	♠ K543	(b)	♠ KJ87	(c)	♠ QJ98	(d)	♠ QJ9876
	♥ 864		♥ A73		♥ J63		♥ 5
	♦ A62		♦ 6		♦ 42		♦ A5
	♣ 643		♣ 87654		♣ KJ64		♣ 6432

(a) Bid 3D – Showing Preference to opener's first suit.

(b) Bid 3H – Showing Preference to opener's second suit.

(c) Bid 2NT – holding two stoppers in the un-bid suit and unwilling to play in either of opener's suits.

(d) Bid 2S – re-bidding your own suit. This promises a 6-card suit, and no liking for either of partner's suits.

All of these re-bids show minimum hands with no more than 8 or 9pts and, although opener may bid on, he would be well advised to have in excess of the 16pts that he has already promised.

If you are stronger – 10pts or more – then, opposite a promised 16pts, you should be heading for Game.

II WITH STRONGER HANDS

Opener bid 1D, you responded 1S, and opener re-bids 2H:

(a) ♠ KQJ3   (b) ♠ KQ872   (c) ♠ AQJ752 (d) ♠ QJ98
   ♥ 8   ♥ A732   ♥ 5   ♥ J63
   ♦ A862   ♦ Q   ♦ A5   ♦ A2
   ♣ 6432   ♣ 843   ♣ 6432   ♣ KJ64

(a) Bid 4D. Jump-support opener's first suit.

(b) Bid 4H. Jump to Game in opener's second suit.

(c) Bid 3S. A jump re-bid in your own suit promises 6 cards, and is forcing.

(d) Bid 3NT. Two stoppers in the un-bid suit.

    With only one stopper, bid 4th Suit Forcing (see page 57).

*With 10pts or more opposite a reverse you
must take strong action which will result in a Game contract.*

Conclusions – Two Key Principles
Despite all the various complicated responder's re-bids you may choose, two simple rules will steer you into the right spot most of the time. Hence they should be at the forefront of your mind:

*If three suits have been bid, and you then bid NTs,
you are promising TWO stoppers in the un-bid suit.
And
If you hold an opening hand opposite an opening hand
your final contract should be Game.*

RESPONDER'S RE-BIDS

SHOW PREFERENCE
(between partner's suits)

when you hold a minimum for your initial response. Always return partner to his first suit, unless you hold two more cards in his second suit than in his first.

SUPPORT PARTNER

when you know you have an 8-card fit. Raise to the 2-level with 6–9pts, the 3-level with 10–12pts, and Game with 13pts+. After a reverse: Show Preference with 6–8pts, and raise to Game with a good 9pts or more.

BID NTs

6–9pts = 1NT, 10–12pts = 2NT, 13–15pts = 3NT. After a reverse: bid 3NT on 10pts+. When three suits have been bid, you guarantee TWO stoppers in the un-bid suit.

RE-BID YOUR SUIT

to show a 6-card suit. A minimum level re-bid is encouraging, but not forcing. With 11pts or more, jump in the suit, or consider bidding the fourth suit.

BID THE FOURTH SUIT

"Fourth Suit Forcing" – forcing partner to continue describing his hand. At the 1- and 2-levels, your suit may just be small cards; at the 3-level, partner will assume you hold one stopper in the suit.

There are several **forcing** bids at this stage in the auction. These are the two most important ones:

Bid the fourth suit – 4SF (see page 57)
Bid a <u>new</u> suit at the 3-level

7

PRE-EMPTIVE BIDDING

Opening Pre-empts

A pre-emptive opening bid of 3C, 3D, 3H or 3S is intended to use up the opponents' bidding space so that they misjudge the level, and even the correct suit, in which they should be playing.

The standard hand for this bid is one containing a high-quality 7-card suit, with *fewer* than 10 HCP.

Also, because you are risking a penalty – being doubled by your opponents and failing by two or three tricks – in return for pushing up the bidding to barrage them, it is essential that you hold as few defensive tricks outside your long suit as possible.

Take these hands as examples:

♠ A865432   Many players would incorrectly open 3S. But
♥ Q4   there is no point using up your opponents' bidding
♦ Q7   space because, even if they reach a contract
♣ Q8   of 4H, your A♠ and Queens make your hand
            very suitable for defence. Whereas, if you
are doubled for penalties in 3S, your hand is unlikely to
produce more than four tricks.

♠ KQJ9876   Here, your hand will definitely produce six tricks
♥ 2   if played in spades, but is unlikely to produce
♦ 842   any tricks if defending the opponents' contract.
♣ 82   For this reason, it is worth the risk of a penalty
               to try to stop them from finding the correct
Game contract. If your partner holds a strong hand, and bids
on, he will not be disappointed by your strong spades.

So, remember:

*Before partner has had a chance to bid, you deny any Aces
outside the suit in which you are pre-empting.*

Most importantly, the quality of your long suit should be
good, especially as you are making a pre-judgement before
your partner has had a chance to bid. There is little more frus-
trating than to hold a beautiful hand only to hear partner pre-
empt before you have had a chance to bid. For that reason, it
is important to promise a minimum suit quality when you are
bidding before your partner:

*Your suit should be headed by three of the five honours,
including either the Ace or the King.*

Knowing this, at least partner will be able to judge whether to
bid on, and to what contract, with some degree of certainty.
However:

*Once partner has already passed, your range for a pre-empt can
be wider (a little weaker, or a little stronger), your suit quality
may be slightly poorer, and you may have an outside Ace.*

This is because, since partner has passed, you cannot spoil his
good hand. The only auction you will be spoiling now is your
opponents' – and that is just what you want to do.

Whilst this barrage technique plays an essential role in all good bidding, it is vital that the possible gains of the bid are weighed carefully against the risk. For this reason, when vulnerable, you will need to be a little stronger than when not.

When non-vulnerable, you should be prepared to go three down if left in the pre-empt contract but, when vulnerable, two down is as many as you should be prepared to fail by.

Weak 3 Openers
Let's look at some examples of the thinking thus far:

(a) ♠ KQJ9876   (b) ♠ A4   (c) ♠ 9
♥ –   ♥ KQJ8654   ♥ 6
♦ J98   ♦ 632   ♦ AQJ9876
♣ 765   ♣ 2   ♣ Q432

(a) Open 3S. You expect to make six tricks so this is perfect for a non-vulnerable opening. Indeed, as the shape is so good, 3S would be acceptable vulnerable as well.

(b) Open 1H. You are far too strong for a pre-empt, and the outside Ace precludes you from even considering it.

(c) Open 3D, vulnerable or not. The excellent shape and lack of major suits means that a pre-empt is highly advisable. If you are feeling aggressive, 4D is quite reasonable not vulnerable.

Weak 4 Openers
An opening bid of 4C, 4D, 4H, or 4S is weak also, showing a 7- or 8-card suit and little else. Follow the same rules as for the Weak 3's in terms of how many tricks you are prepared to go down by at each vulnerability. Most players regard the restriction on outside Aces and Kings as being lifted.

5 Openers

5C or 5D as opening bids are usually fairly weak. After all, if you hold 11 tricks in your hand, you are so close to a slam that you should be opening 2C. (See page 75.)

5C or 5D openers usually consist of an 8 or 9-card suit, with an outside value elsewhere. It is quite common for one of these pre-empts to be bid and played, quietly go two off, and for the opponents then to discover that they had a slam available in a major suit. That, of course, is the whole point of the pre-empt. It is not easy to enter the bidding at the 5-level!

5H or 5S as opening bids have a slightly different meaning. In Acol these are slam-going conventional bids to show that you can make all the tricks in your own hand, except for the top two trump tricks. On a hand like this:

♠ QJ109865	You should open 5S, which asks partner to bid
♥ –	6S if he holds either A♠ or K♠, and to bid 7S if
♦ AKQJ7	he holds both top honours. Once your partner
♣ A	is known to hold ♠AK, you cannot lose a trick.

If only hands like this cropped up a little more often...

Responding to Opening Pre-empts

This is comparatively easy, because you know what your partner is promising you. He knows that you require from him a minimum suit quality if you have not yet had a chance to bid; thus you can judge the likely number of tricks available to the partnership.

If you have already passed, you will want to pass again.

If you have not yet passed, and you decide that you are worth a bid, remember that:

Opposite a major-suit pre-empt, support partner;
opposite a minor suit, your eye should be firmly on NTs.

There are three main actions you can take:

I RAISE PARTNER

Remembering that partner holds a high-quality 7-card suit is the most important thing. A singleton is therefore adequate support.

♠ K
♥ AK543
♦ A743
♣ 743

Partner opens 3S, non-vulnerable. He is expecting to make six tricks, so with your four tricks you should have the ten you need for Game. With seven spades opposite you, your K♠ should be just what partner wants, so bid 4S.

II BID 3NT

This bid is nearly always made on the wrong hands.

It is essential that you have a fit with partner's suit in order to bid 3NT in response to a pre-empt.

If you do not have a fit with partner, you may well find it impossible to get into partner's hand at all.

In each case partner has opened 3D, and you hold:

(a) ♠ AQ3
     ♥ K5
     ♦ K85
     ♣ AJ532

(b) ♠ KQ5
     ♥ AQ87
     ♦ 2
     ♣ K5432

(c) ♠ A73
     ♥ A52
     ♦ A743
     ♣ A82

(a) Bid 3NT – a classic raise to 3NT. You have stoppers in each suit and, with your K♦, partner's diamonds should produce seven tricks now. A slam is a long way off, whilst 3NT should be an easy Game.

(b) Pass. Completely wrong to bid 3NT. Partner cannot hold solid diamonds or he would have opened 3NT (see page 71) and, because partner has guaranteed weakness outside his suit, you will be unable to get into partner's hand in any other suit. 3NT is likely to go three or four down, maybe doubled.

(c) Bid 3NT. Perfect for the bid. Partner's six tricks opposite your four will be enough for 3NT, but not enough for 5D. Once more, this shows the advantage of playing in NTs rather than a minor suit.

III CHANGE THE SUIT

A change of suit opposite a pre-empt is 100 per cent forcing: never do it as a "rescue". This is a Game-going bid, made with a suit which you regard as a genuine alternative to your partner's 7-card offering. This change of suit usually occurs after a minor suit pre-empt, when the responder holds a good 6-card major suit.

♠ AQ8543   Partner opens 3D, and you respond 3S, hoping
♥ AK5   for a 4S contract. If partner holds ♠Jx or three
♦ 8   small spades he will probably raise to 4S. If he
♣ K43   has a singleton or void in spades, he will re-bid
               4D, which, unless you are feeling particularly
               frisky, you should pass.

♠ AKQJ87   Opposite 3D, this time you should bid 4S
♥ AK5   immediately. You do not need help in spades
♦ –   from partner, and all you can do is hope that
♣ K753   he holds Q♥, Q♣, or ♣J10 to help you on your
               way.

After a jump *to Game* the opener should pass.

Opposite all opening pre-empts, you should remember that:

When responding to pre-empts, you should take note only of your Aces and Kings.

Partners who pre-empt are not interested in Queens and Jacks. They usually hold only one or two cards in each of the outside suits, so it is the controls which are important to them. Once again, count the tricks.

3NT Opening Bid
This is known as the "Acol Gambling 3NT". However, it is a gamble pretty much in your favour, since it combines the opportunity of barraging the opponents, with making a slim Game contract – in comparative safety.

This opening bid shows a *solid* (headed by AKQJ) 7-card minor suit, with no more than one King outside this suit. 13 HCP should be your maximum. If you are any stronger, you should be opening with a Strong 2. (See page 82.)

In response, if partner has a chance of a few tricks, he will pass, and allow you to play in 3NT. Your solid minor suit will provide seven tricks and you hope that you can pick up the other two somewhere along the line.

If partner is very weak, or you are doubled in 3NT and partner cannot stand it, he will bid 4C. If this is your suit you pass; if not, you convert to 4D.

In this contract you must make at least seven tricks, plus 100 or 150pts for honours if you are playing Rubber bridge, whereas your opponents could almost certainly have made a Game contract with another suit as trumps. The worst loss you can possibly endure – if vulnerable and pushed to 4C or 4D – would be three off for 800pts, minus 100 or 150pts for honours. This seems bad but, if partner cannot provide a single trick for you, it seems likely your opponents have a slam on. Most often, 4C or 4D goes one down, and turns out to be an excellent save against your opponents making Game. After all, if you only hold 12 or 13 HCP, and partner is terribly weak, then your opponents must have Game on.

You sit West on these hands:

West	East
♠ Q65	♠ J8
♥ 76	♥ A43
♦ AKQJ1087	♦ 54
♣ 5	♣ A86432

You open 3NT, and partner, with two certain tricks, can afford to risk the spade position and pass. As it happens, even on a spade lead, 3NT is fine.

West	East
♠ 76	♠ 543
♥ K7	♥ 963
♦ AKQJ874	♦ 93
♣ 83	♣ AKQ76

You open 3NT, but partner with two suits completely unguarded should not leave 3NT to play. You cannot have a high card in both spades and hearts. Instead, he can bid 4D – it must be your suit. 4D will only fail if all the cards are wrong, and the defence is very accurate. 3NT will almost certainly fail and, if the cards are badly placed and the defence is timed perfectly, you may lose the first nine or ten tricks.

8

STRONG OPENING BIDS AND RESPONSES

With 20pts+, or 8 playing tricks +, in your hand, it is time to consider opening the bidding at the 2-level.

The most important rule to remember when considering a strong opening bid is:

With a balanced hand, count your points. With a distributional hand, count your tricks.

2NT Opening

This shows a balanced hand with a good 20–22pts.

What is a "good" 20pts?

Well, you are only opening the bidding at the 2-level because you are afraid that, if you open at the 1-level and partner passes, you might be missing Game.

Take these hands, for examples:

(a)   ♠ A754   (b) ♠ QJ9
      ♥ AK3   ♥ AJ10
      ♦ KQ   ♦ AKJ75
      ♣ A532   ♣ A7

(a) If 20pts can ever be horrible, then this is it.

   If partner is so weak that he would be passing a 1-level opening, then you certainly won't want to be playing in 2NT. The hand contains five tricks and that's it.

   Just open 1C and, if partner passes, you will be better off than in 2NT; if he responds, now you can re-bid 3NT, showing 19/20pts.

(b) This is much better, and should certainly be opened with 2NT. The ♥AJ10 will probably produce two tricks, and the 5-card diamond suit will also be good value. You won't need much from partner to make 2NT, and only a bit more than that to make 3NT.

Whilst we're on the subject of length in NT contracts, don't forget that:

AKQ   is 9pts, and will make three tricks, whilst
AKQ432   is also 9pts, but will probably make six tricks.

So, length – especially in a minor suit – should be prized in NT contracts.

   All the following hands are suitable for a 2NT opening:

(a)	♠ AQ5	(b)	♠ AQ	(c)	♠ KQJ43
	♥ J6		♥ AQ		♥ A54
	♦ KQJ98		♦ QJ765		♦ KJ8
	♣ AKJ		♣ KQJ4		♣ AK

(a) Do not worry about the poor doubleton heart.

(b) Not strictly a balanced hand but, with excellent holdings in the majors, 2NT looks the only sensible opening.

(c) A 5-card major of any quality is quite acceptable in a 2NT opening, especially if you are playing Modified Baron responses. (See page 150.)

As in hand (b), not all 2NT openings will be on strictly balanced hands. A 6-card minor is often acceptable, and 5–4 distribution is quite common. To open 2NT on these strong hands is not perfect. However, it is simply the best way to deal with them.

Responses to 2NT
The responses to 2NT are consistent in meaning with those for 1NT, without the 2-level Weak Take-Out responses.

All bids opposite 2NT are forcing to Game.

Any bid will show at least 5pts, so that the combined point count is in the Game range (25–32pts). Compare these response meanings with responses to 1NT in Chapter 3:

3NT	denotes a balanced hand, or one containing a long minor suit, with 5–10pts.
3C	is Stayman (page 22) or Modified Baron (page 150).
3D	is a slam try.
3H, 3S	show 5-card suits, and are Game forcing.
4H, 4S	show 6-card suits, or longer.

2C Opening
This is a conventional (artificial) opening bid, showing a very strong hand. With a single exception, explained on page 79, it is forcing to Game.

Many players are under the misapprehension that to open 2C always requires 23 HCP or more. This is untrue.

There are two types of 2C Opening, depending on what shape of hand you hold:

With a suitable Distributional hand, you open 2C, and then re-bid <u>a suit</u>.

With an appropriate Balanced hand, you open 2C, and then re-bid <u>NTs</u>.

Let's take each in turn:

I DISTRIBUTIONAL HANDS

When deciding whether to open the bidding with 2C, you must count the number of "Playing Tricks" your hand contains. (See page 83.)

If the total is 8–9½, then open 2 of your suit. (See page 83.)

However, if you have 9 certain tricks when playing in No-trumps, open 2C.

With 10 potential tricks or more, you should open the bidding with 2C, and then re-bid your suit.

This tells partner that you believe you hold <u>Game in your own hand</u>, and that you have a 6-card suit (or longer) or, possibly, 5–5 distribution (or greater).

(a)	♠ AKQ10976	(b)	♠ AKQ62	(c)	♠ A75
	♥ AKQ		♥ AKQJ4		♥ K3
	♦ 74		♦ A9		♦ AKQ9542
	♣ 2		♣ 2		♣ A

(a) The hand contains 10 tricks if spades are trumps. Open 2C, and re-bid 2S over partner's response. Whatever he bids next, re-bid spades to show him you hold a 1-suited hand.

(b) Again, 10 potential tricks, but you wish to find your best trump fit. Open 2C, re-bid 2S, and if partner does not support you, bid 3H next.

(c) You have only 20pts but, unless the diamonds split exceptionally badly, you will make 3NT. It will be most effective to open this hand with 2C and then rebid 3NT (showing 25–27pts). Even if your partner bids on, he will not be disappointed that you have fewer points, since you will supply him with easy tricks. Do not open 2D, or 2C followed by a diamond re-bid, since this will make finding 3NT much more difficult.

Notice that hand (a) has only 18 HCP, and hand (c) only 20. Both are clear-cut 2C openers, so bang goes that 23pts theory! Look again at hand (c) – opposite nothing at all in partner's hand Game in 3NT will almost certainly make. However 0pts opposite a balanced hand of say, 26pts, would not get close to making Game in 3NT. So, hand (c) is much stronger than a 26pt balanced hand.

Remember that:

Having opened 2C you never re-bid 4-card suits.
You must be in a position to re-bid a 6-card suit,
or the first of a 5–5 distribution or better.

Partner will be happy to support your suit on three small cards, or even a doubleton honour.

A rare but important bid is the jump re-bid by a 2C opener. As the whole point of opening 2C is so that you can subsequently bid slowly, when you jump it has a special meaning.

2C – 2D   You open 2C; partner responds 2D – the
<u>3H</u>   negative. Your jump re-bid of 3H shows a
    completely solid suit in which you require no
♠ A4   support. This bid sets the suit without argu-
♥ AKQJ109   ment, and the partnership can immediately
♦ 98   Cue-bid (see page 118), or use Blackwood to
♣ AKQ   investigate slam possibilities. (See page 132.)
    As this hand shows, even if partner is void in
    hearts, you won't mind.

II BALANCED HANDS

With balanced hands you are only concerned with a point count. And now a minimum of 23pts *is* required for 2C.

With 23/24 HCP, open 2C, and re-bid 2NT.
With 25–27 HCP, open 2C, and re-bid 3NT.

These are limit re-bids, and partner may choose to pass, raise NTs, or show 5- or 6-card major suits in response. Yes, partner may pass 2NT. It is the one 2C sequence that he is permitted to pass before Game is reached. If you have 23/24pts, and he holds a Yarborough (no points whatsoever), why do you want to be in more than 2NT?

Agreed beforehand, a regular partnership may also play Stayman (see page 22), or Modified Baron (see page 150) in response to a 2NT re-bid.

Most importantly, having made either limit NT re-bid, you have described your hand perfectly so the decision of whether to go for a slam lies entirely with your partner.

Bridge is all about making good decisions on the hands which don't fit into the text-book definitions. So here, in a fearless attempt to anticipate problem hands, are a couple of close decisions other text-books would rather not tackle...

(a) ♠ AKQJ4   (b) ♠ A7
    ♥ A64   ♥ K8
    ♦ AJ4   ♦ AKQJ987
    ♣ AJ   ♣ A3

On hand (a) you merrily open 2C. Partner responds 2D and, with such strength in spades, you are just about to re-bid 2S, when you realize that this would show 10 Playing Tricks, which you have not got... In other words, this hand qualifies for a 2C opener as a balanced hand (23 HCP+), but is way short if you want to re-bid your spade suit.

Much better than a sub-standard 2S opening (you ought to have a 6-card suit), I suggest you treat it as 24pts balanced; open 2C, and re-bid 2NT. Then, playing Modified Baron (see page 150), there is no danger of missing a spade fit.

Hand (b) looks like a 2D opener (9½ Playing Tricks – see page 83 – and a good suit), but a partner holding no tricks will pass, and you may be left in a part score whilst holding a hand on which 3NT will always make. The hand may only have 21 HCP but, with the long diamond suit, it is really worth about 25/26pts; so, treat it as a 2C balanced hand opener and re-bid 3NT. If partner bids on, he won't be disappointed to see your hand.

The way to avoid problems with these difficult hands is to think of your re-bid <u>before</u> opening in the first place. But that is just good play anyway…

Responses to 2C
A 2C opener is forcing to Game – the only exception being when the opener re-bids 2NT, showing 23/24pts. Then, if you hold 0 or 1pt, you may pass. Otherwise, you have to keep bidding.

In the old days, players thought it important for the responder to a 2C opener to reveal immediately what he held. In fact, until you know what type of 2C opener your partner holds, there is probably little advantage in telling him about your hand, unless you can guarantee him a definite source of tricks. For that reason, for the vast majority of the time, you should respond to 2C with a bid of 2D.

This 2D response is played as a "relay" – a bid simply to keep the auction running – allowing the 2C opener to describe his hand. With that information, responder can judge whether or not his values will be of use to his partner.

If, however, you hold a truly dreadful hand (no Aces, no Kings and no more than one Queen) then, if the opener rebids a suit, you should be ready with a <u>second negative</u>: a rebid of No-trumps at the lowest available level. This tells your partner that you are extra super awful.

	West	East
(a)	♠ A9	♠ J7543
	♥ AKQJ75	♥ 32
	♦ AKQ	♦ 98
	♣ 85	♣ 7432
	2C	2D
	2H	2NT
	4H	NB

You respond 2D initially, and re-bid 2NT to show an extra bad hand. Partner then forgets any slams ambitions and settles for game in 4H.

	West	East
(b)	♠ QJ7	♠ K86432
	♥ AKQ8	♥ J5
	♦ AKQ5	♦ J4
	♣ Q4	♣ 975
	2C	2D
	2NT	4S
	NB	

You respond 2D again but, when partner re-bids 2NT, showing 23/24pts, you can now jump to 4S, showing a weak-ish hand with a 6-card spade suit.

Even with as many as 9 or 10pts, you should still respond 2D since, if partner subsequently shows a wild, distributional hand, your values may be of limited use. If, instead, he shows a balanced hand, you can then raise him in no-trumps.

2D, then, is played as a relay bid and not as a negative (although you could be very weak).

To respond to 2C with any other bid is a positive response, indicating a 5-card suit or longer headed by two of the top three honour cards: AK, AQ, or KQ. Although this means that you will only rarely give a positive response, when you do, your partner knows exactly where your tricks lie and he can judge if they will be of use to him. Remember that, once 2C has been opened, no one bids 4-card suits. If you have a strong hand with a high-quality 4-card suit, simply relay with a 2D response and, if partner rebids 2NT, you will still have Stayman to discover a 4-4 major-suit fit. (This is the one time anyone would bid a 4-card suit after a 2C opener.)

This hand came up in a big tournament. My partner and I bid the slam with ease. Although some other pairs also reached it, they took many more bids and suffered much more angst:

West	East
♠ KJ4	♠ AQ753
♥ A4	♥ 853
♦ AKQJ962	♦ 84
♣ A	♣ J92
2C	2S
7NT	

Whoah! A grand slam in three bids? How did that happen?

When my partner opened 2C, I responded with a positive 2S. This promised a 5-card suit or longer, headed by two of the top three honours. Partner realized that, with his ♠KJ, we had a certain five spade tricks, seven diamonds, A♥ and A♣. That made fourteen tricks! So, it was easy to bid the grand.

RESPONSES TO 2C OPENING BID

Initial Responses
With no high quality 5-card suit or longer,
regardless of point-count, respond: 2D

If you hold a 5-card suit or longer, headed
by two of the top three honour cards
(AK, AQ or KQ), then bid your suit   2H or 2S,
immediately in response to the 2C opener: 3C or 3D

Responder's Re-bids After a 2C Opener
If you hold a very weak hand, with no Ace,
King, and no more than one Queen, having
responded 2D initially, if opener re-bids
a suit, you must re-bid: 2NT

Otherwise, bid a 5-card (or longer) major
suit, or if the 2C opener re-bids 2NT,
Stayman can be used to seek a 4-4 major-
suit fit.

If you hold a weak hand, and partner
re-bids no-trumps, simply pass (with 0 or 1pt),
or raise partner.

Strong 2 Openers: 2D 2H 2S

Because we are dealing with strong <u>distributional</u> hands,
points are irrelevant. Both you and partner are interested
solely in <u>tricks</u>.

Before moving on to the opening bids and responses, let's
revise our thoughts on **Playing Tricks**.

You assess how many tricks your suit is worth by assuming
that the outstanding cards in the suit are distributed equally

between your partner and each of the opponents. For the purposes of this evaluation, you discount the rare occasions when one opponent may hold many or all of the remaining cards – if you are too pessimistic, you will never bid anything:

AKQJ   will obviously produce 4 tricks.

AKQJ32   should produce 6 tricks, <u>in the play</u>. By the time you have played the top four honours, the small cards will be good.

AK65432   should produce at least 5 tricks.

AQ   1½ Playing Tricks. The holding makes 2 tricks when the finesse wins, and only 1 when it loses.

AQJ   2½ tricks. Whether Q wins or loses J is a definite trick. So, consider you hold 1½ for AQ, plus certain tricks for all the next cards in sequence.

K53   is taken to be ½ trick. K makes half the time.

KQ3   is presumed to be 1½ tricks. Q always makes here, and K makes half the time.

KQJ765   is more difficult to assess, and views will differ. 4½ or 5 Playing Tricks seems about right.

AJ8532   another difficult suit – perhaps worth 3½ or 4 tricks.

Assessing Playing Tricks is not an exact science. Expert players come up with different answers. Above all, it is better to be a little over-optimistic than the other way around.

Your requirements to open a Strong 2 are as follows:

A high quality 6-card suit +,
combined with 8–9½ Playing Tricks.

Remember that, with 10 Playing Tricks in your hand, you have Game in your own hand, and should open the bidding with 2C.

(a)	♠ AKQJ106	(b)	♠ A4	(c)	♠ 642
	♥ AJ6		♥ AKQJ97		♥ AKQJ874
	♦ A73		♦ Q83		♦ –
	♣ 2		♣ 42		♣ AK4

(a) A bare-minimum 2S opener including just 8 Playing Tricks.

(b) Only 7 Playing Tricks, so this is not good enough for 2H. Open 1H and, if partner responds, plan to jump re-bid 3H.

(c) A near-maximum 2H opener. 9 Playing Tricks; good shape.

Reserve Strong 2 openers for 1-suited hands.

2-suited hands, even when strong, are best opened at the 1-level, followed by a jump re-bid in the second suit.

(a)	♠ AKQJ6	(b)	♠ AKQJ98	(c)	♠ AKQJ74
	♥ AQ854		♥ 5		♥ 2
	♦ Q7		♦ AKJ43		♦ K4
	♣ 6		♣ 4		♣ AK76

(a) Open 1S; unless partner supports, plan to re-bid 3H.

(b) Open 2C. You have 10 Playing Tricks – 6 in hearts, 4 in diamonds.

(c) Open 2S. Ignore 4-card minor. Treat this as a 1-suited hand.

Responses to Strong 2 Openers: 2D 2H 2S

Traditionally, it has been usual to play a Strong 2 Opener as forcing for one round. In the more logical modern Acol this is not the case. After all, if partner is promising 8 tricks, and is bidding at the 2-level, it would be ridiculous to push him to the 3-level if you have no trick in your hand.

For this reason, with no chance of taking a single trick in your hand, you are permitted to pass. Please remember that you can only do this if you think your hand will not contribute a *single* trick.

Let's take a look at these examples. Your partner opens 2H. Should you pass on any of these hands?

(a)	♠ 8532	(b)	♠ 5	(c)	♠ KJ7
	♥ 5		♥ 8742		♥ 85
	♦ J864		♦ 86432		♦ 97542
	♣ 6432		♣ 963		♣ J52

(a) Yes, pass. Genuinely no chance of providing a trick. If J♦ turns out to be the one card partner needs, too bad.

(b) No. You are far too good to pass, as you hold 4-card support and a singleton spade. Partner may be able to make two or three spade ruffs in your hand.

(c) No. ♠KJ7 is likely to be one trick, and may be two.

What you should respond on hands (b) and (c) is 2NT. This is the official negative response, which tells partner that you think you have one trick in your hand, and just possibly two or more. If he has a minimum he will re-bid his suit at the 3-level, and you will probably pass. If he has opened with 9 or 9½ tricks, then he will jump to Game in his suit.

Any other response to a Strong 2 opener is forcing to Game.

As partner has a high quality 6-card suit, you only require a doubleton honour or three small cards in that suit, to support your partner straightaway. There are two different supporting bids you can make. Assuming partner opens 2H, you can respond 3H or 4H.

Both bids show a doubleton honour, or 3-cards+, trump support. Both bids show that you have at least 2 tricks in your hand.

BUT

3H – the single raise – promises at least one Ace or a void somewhere in the hand, whereas,

4H – the jump raise – denies an Ace or a void anywhere.

The reason for this peculiarity has to do with bidding space.

Without an Ace or void in your hand, chances of a slam are small, so you might as well jump to Game, expecting partner to pass. (If he holds all the Aces he'll probably bid on…)

With Aces or voids in your hand, there may well be a slam, and by keeping the bidding lower, it allows more space to investigate, using Cue-bids. (See page 139.)

Only when you cannot support your partner should you show your own suit. In doing so, partner will expect you not only to hold two tricks, but also a good quality 5-card suit or longer, and may raise you with 3-card support.

Any suit you mention should be one which you genuinely think is a viable trump-suit alternative to partner's high quality 6-card suit. There is no need to jump in your suit, because your response itself, as stated earlier, is already forcing to Game.

When partner opens the bidding with 2D, both of you should have an eye on 3NT as the final contract. (Remembering that, with a long minor, you should still always be heading for NTs if possible.) So, with some useful cards in the outside suits, and at least two diamonds in your hand, you can certainly consider responding 3NT to an opening 2D bid.

Your partner opens 2H. What should you respond on these hands?

(a) ♠ AJ975   (b) ♠ KQJ853   (c) ♠ KJ76
    ♥ K75   ♥ 4   ♥ K7
    ♦ Q43   ♦ Q43   ♦ 97532
    ♣ 82   ♣ 852   ♣ 95

(a) 3H, promising an Ace or a void in the hand. Do not mention your spades. ♥Kxx is excellent support, and that together with A♠ is worth at least two tricks.

(b) 2S. You dislike hearts this time, and a spade contract may well be best.

(c) 4H, denying an Ace or void. ♥Kx is very good support.

Sometimes there is confusion over who should push on to a slam. The basic rule is that, when you have described your hand fully to your partner, you must let him make up his mind as to what the final contract should be. If you open with a Strong 2 and then re-bid, you will have described your hand in detail. Your partner will know the length of your suit, and the number of tricks your hand contains. Therefore, it should be he who chooses whether to bid on towards a slam contract.

STRONG 2 OPENERS

To open 2D 2H 2S, you require both:

A high quality 6-card suit, or longer and 8–9½ Playing Tricks.

N.B. How many points you hold is irrelevant.

RESPONSES TO STRONG 2 OPENERS

No chance of a trick	NB
One trick likely; two or more tricks possible Negative response	2NT
Doubleton honour or 3-cards+ trump support and two tricks or more with at least one Ace or void	Single Raise
As above, but NO Ace or void	Jump Raise
Less than 3-cards or doubleton honour trump support as above, but two tricks + and good quality 5-card suit, or longer	Show suit
(Opposite 2D Opener) Scattering of values in outside suits At least 2-card support for diamonds	3NT, to play

9

COMPETITIVE BIDDING

Now that you – and possibly your opponents too – are bidding much more accurately, it is time to consider spoiling their science, with a bit of *action*.

The dual purposes of the bids included in this chapter are to obstruct your opponents in their quest for the best contract, and to bully your way into the auction, possibly stealing the contract in the process.

This will make you harder to play against, enhance your final scores, and bring you added enjoyment as you will be able to enter the auction on weaker types of hand.

Once someone opens the bidding – that is, makes a positive bid – the role of each player is cast in stone for the remainder of the hand. The opener's partner is the responder, and the opponents are the overcallers.

As an overcaller, there are three main actions you can take once an opponent has opened the bidding. They are:

(i)   Overcalling, at various levels.
(ii) Double.
(iii) Pass.

All of these actions have fairly specific meanings, but pass is what you will do first most often, either because you hold a poor hand, or because, despite quite a few points, your hand is unsuitable for any other action <u>at that moment</u>.

It is most important to remember that with a suitable hand – even one with only a very few points – it is still possible to enter the bidding, both to disrupt the opponents' bidding sequence and/or to pinpoint the best lead. Even players with poor cards can threaten a good run for the opponents, and that should always be the basis of your tactics.

> *Score with good cards as many points as you can;*
> *lose as few as possible with poor ones,*
> *by barraging your opponents into the wrong contract.*

In competition bridge, all the experts have realized that it is easier to stop your opponents from reaching the right contract, than it is successfully to defend against it once they've got there. So, barraging your opponents with pre-emptive openings and overcalls is even more popular today than ever, and is a vital part of the system.

Let's take a long look at each of the options to get you into the action after an opponent has opened the bidding:

Overcalls

An overcall is usually a weak bid.

Often you hold fewer HCPs than on a hand with which you would pass. It is your hand's shape which makes it worth a bid. Signalling that shape, however, is the whole idea of an overcall. It is not the start of a "conversation"; it is a <u>Newsflash</u> of information, based on a good quality suit.

You should make an overcall for at least one, and preferably both, of these reasons:

(a) To suggest a suit in which you and your partner might try to barrage your opponents.

(b) To suggest a good lead to partner.

As with a pre-emptive opening bid, you are not necessarily expecting to make the contract you bid, but you are hoping that you will use up your opponents' bidding space and that, once they reach their contract, partner will (where appropriate) find the best lead of your suit.

Simple Overcall
A Simple Overcall is an overcall in your suit at the lowest available level. It is the overcall which you will use by far the most, and the one which can have the greatest impact on your opponents, whilst exposing you to the least risk.

The text-book requirements are as follows:

(a) A high quality 5-card suit, or longer, probably headed by three of the five honours, including either the Ace or King. At the 1-level (i.e. 1D, 1S) a minimum of 8pts.

(b) At the 2-level (i.e. 1D, 2C), a minimum of 10/11pts with a high-quality 6-card suit or 12pts with a high-quality 5-card suit.

Your RHO (right hand opponent) opens 1D. It would be correct to overcall on each of the following hands:

(a) ♠ AQJ98   (b) ♠ 2   (c) ♠ 86
    ♥ J5   ♥ AKQ95   ♥ AJ7
    ♦ 9532   ♦ A53   ♦ 53
    ♣ 94   ♣ 8532   ♣ KQJ986

(a) A minimum overcall of 1S.

(b) A stronger hand, but a Simple Overcall of 1H is the best bid.

(c) An overcall of 2C prevents the responder from bidding at the 1-level, and should attract the best lead from your partner.

When defining the requirements for a Simple Overcall, I deliberately referred just above to the "text-book" requirements. This is because the situation can be quite different in a book compared with at the table. The former is relaxed; the latter is war!

The prime reason for overcalling is to obstruct your opponents, and so it should follow that the more obstructive the overcall is, the less you require to make it. In other words, the more you stand to gain by bidding, the greater a risk you can afford to take. For example:

♠ AJ987 Over an opening bid of 1H, you should pass.
♥ 86   There is no point sticking your neck out with a
♦ J1098 sub-minimum hand when an overcall of 1S will
♣ 53   not upset your opponents at all. Does 1H – 1S
         prevent responder from making his planned
         response? Not at all.

Over an opening bid of 1C or 1D, however, you should overcall 1S. Your spade suit is 5-card, with good intermediate cards. If the responder was planning to bid 1H, he will now have to move to the 2-level. The opener's re-bid may also be affected. If your partner can bid 2S, opener would have to find a second bid in any suit, at the 3-level. Now, your opponents, who probably hold the majority of points, are the ones under pressure.

So, the more you can upset your opponents, the weaker you can be.

Vulnerability

Before looking at some of the other overcalls, and their responses, we must pause for a moment to consider the aspect of vulnerability.

If you are vulnerable, an overcall becomes a much more dangerous action because, if your opponents are faced with a decision to bid on in their suit or to double you in your contract, they will be much more inclined to double and take the penalty points from defeating you.

This effect is maximized when you are vulnerable but your opponents are not.

The various comparative vulnerabilities are summed up by the following terms, which serve also to indicate the relative dangers:

Favourable: You are non-vulnerable; your opponents are.
Equal: The vulnerability is the same for both sides.
Adverse: You are vulnerable; your opponents are not.

Favourable overcalls are the safest; your opponents having to weigh up the opportunity to make Game and rubber (or a vulnerable Game at Duplicate or Teams) against the relatively few points above the line they might earn via a non-vulnerable penalty double. Quite often they will push on ill-advisedly, rather than doubling you.

The bottom line is that all overcalls involve some degree of risk. If yours do not, then you are not overcalling enough on marginal hands. If the length and suit quality you hold are up to scratch you are pretty safe, but if there is a close decision you should consider carefully the comparative vulnerabilities.

For example, your RHO opens 1D, and you hold:

♠ Q53   If you are non-vulnerable, you might risk an over-
♥ 74   call of 2C. Even though your suit quality is marginal
♦ A42   and you have minimum values, the bid does cut
♣ AQ973   out both 1-level major suit responses for your
          opponents. If vulnerable, the risk is too great, and
          you should probably pass.

It is almost impossible to legislate absolutely about overcalls. Much will be decided by your judgement of your opponents, partner, and the state of the game. That judgement comes only from awareness that grows with practice.

From my experience, I have found that if your suit is spades it is worth taking extra risks to get into the auction. Being the highest ranking suit, it always causes the most obstruction...

Responses to Simple Overcalls
Remember that your partner has overcalled on what is probably a weak hand, with only one good suit, and with the intention of obstructing your opponents. Therefore, the majority of responses to his overcall should also be barrages. However, there is a considerable selection of responses available...

I SUPPORTING PARTNER

This is the bid your partner wants to hear most of all, because it means that you are co-operating with the idea of using up your opponents' bidding space.

All bids supporting partner's overcall are weak.

LHO opens 1D; partner overcalls 1S; RHO bids 2C. You hold:

(a)	♠ K64	(b)	♠ K643	(c)	♠ K8643
	♥ 863		♥ 863		♥ 863
	♦ 86		♦ 6		♦ –
	♣ A8532		♣ A8532		♣ A8532

(a) Raise partner to 2S. This shows 3-card support headed by an honour, confirming that you are happy for him to lead his suit.

(b) Jump raise to 3S. This shows 4-card support.

(c) Jump to 4S. This shows 5-card support.

In each example, points having nothing to do with the level to which you raise partner. Each hand is weak, and could have been weaker still. The deciding factor is the number of trumps you hold.

Assuming that partner holds a 5-card suit for his overcall, you should:

> *Raise partner's overcall to the same number of tricks*
> *as you have trumps between you.*

So, if you think you have a total of eight trumps between you, you should raise partner to eight tricks (the 2-level). If you think you have nine trumps, raise to nine tricks (the 3-level), and so on.

Obviously, vulnerability enters the equation too, but generally, if you hold sufficient trumps, your aggression will pay off.

So, in a barrage situation, it is the number of trumps you hold and the distribution of your hand that is important, not your points.

The more trumps you hold, the better it is for your side to <u>play</u> the hand, and the worse it is to <u>defend</u>. Returning to the examples on the previous page, the simple fact is that the more spades you hold between you, the quicker it will be that your opponents will trump in, making your high cards useless.

Imagine that your partner's hand looks like this:

♠ AQJ97   He has overcalled on a bare minimum, with
♥ 94   some shape. Opposite any of the responses
♦ 9752   above, you would be in with a good chance of
♣ J6   making the contract, even though you are not, in
           fact, expecting to make it; you are just bullying
           your opponents.

Much more significantly, your opponents seem to be making 4H each time. On hand (a) you have made it difficult for them to find their 4-4 heart fit. On (b) you have made it almost impossible, and on (c) they will have to guess what to do at the 5-level. They have 25pts between them and they are the side who are suffering.

II UNASSUMING CUE-BID

If all the supporting bids are weak, what happens when you hold a genuinely good hand? Obviously, you cannot just support partner and hope he understands. You must make a different bid, and the easiest is the so-called "Unassuming Cue-bid". This complicated-sounding bid actually just involves calling the opponents' suit at the lowest available level.

What the bid means is that you think that you and your partner hold the majority of the points, and that there might be a Game contract in the offing for your side. In other words, where supporting your partner is crying wolf to make life difficult for your opponents, this bid is saying that you genuinely think your side holds the majority of the values.

LHO opens 1D; partner overcalls 1S; RHO passes. You hold:

♠ K98　　　You respond by bidding 2D – your opponents'
♥ AKQ64　suit. This asks partner to describe his hand
♦ 743　　　further. If he holds a minimum, he must re-bid
♣ Q5　　　his suit at the lowest available level. If he holds a better than minimum hand, he should then describe another feature of his hand.

Let's imagine you hold the hand above, and the bidding has run as before including your 2D Unassuming Cue-bid. Partner has overcalled on any of these hands:

(a)	♠ AQJ76	(b)	♠ AQJ76	(c)	♠ AQJ764
	♥ J75		♥ J7		♥ 8
	♦ 952		♦ 85		♦ 852
	♣ J8		♣ A876		♣ A84

(a) Partner now re-bids 2S to show that he holds a minimum hand. You might pass, or possibly make one further try with 3S. Either way, you stay out of a hopeless Game contract.

(b) Partner this time re-bids 3C. This shows that he overcalled with more than a minimum, and that he holds 5-4 distribution in spades and clubs. This should be all the encouragement you need now to bid 4S.

(c) Partner re-bids 3S. The jump re-bid shows more than a minimum, with a 6-card suit. Again, you raise to Game.

If, after an Unassuming Cue-bid, partner re-bids his suit at the lowest available level, he confirms holding a minimum overcall. Any other action promises extra values.

So, the Unassuming Cue-bid is used to judge whether or not to push on to Game.

It is a particularly important bid, because the point range of an overcall is so wide. Although a Simple Overcall usually shows around 8–12pts, it is possible that with up to 15pts, the best available bid may still be a Simple Overcall.

Even if your opponents have called two suits, you can use the Unassuming Cue-bid. Standard practice is still to bid the opener's suit in this situation.

III NTs

Partner does not particularly want to hear a NT bid, as his overcall has been based on a good suit with some distribution. Never respond NTs just because you do not like your partner's suit. Remember that, unless partner is doubled for penalties, responding to an overcall is a case of "support or shut-up".

If you decide to respond with a NT bid, take note that partner has overcalled, not opened. Your point count should therefore be three or four points higher than usual. A 1NT response to an overcall ought therefore to show a minimum of 10 or 11 pts.

On the assumption that to make 1NT, you need a partnership total of 21–22pts (see page 6), if partner has overcalled with around 9 or 10pts, you will need at least 11pts to hope to make 1NT. Hence, you require the above much higher values than in response to an opening bid.

LHO opened 1D; partner overcalled 1S; RHO passed. You hold:

(a)	♠ 3	(b)	♠ K8	(c)	♠ K43
	♥ K742		♥ 632		♥ K6
	♦ Q532		♦ KQJ8		♦ AQ73
	♣ A843		♣ J983		♣ A542

(a) Pass. Do not respond 1NT just because you dislike spades. Where will you find your tricks in NTs?

(b) 1NT. You have tolerance for partner's suit, and excellent cards in diamonds which might be wasted if you play in spades. If partner was strong for his overcall, he can bid on.

(c) 2D. Use an Unassuming Cue-bid to find out more about partner's hand. If he re-bids 2S to show a minimum, as is likely, you should make a disciplined pass.

IV CHANGE SUIT

This is a very rare move; if you cannot support your partner's overcall, just pass. You might consider a change of suit in these two situations:

(i) You have tolerance for partner's suit (maybe a doubleton honour, or three small cards) but you have a high quality 5- or 6-card suit of your own you would like to suggest.

(ii) Your partner has overcalled with a minor suit and you have a high-quality 5- or 6-card major suit you can show at the same level.

If you do change the suit, it is non-forcing. If partner holds a minimum – even with some tolerance for your suit – he will pass. For this reason, you should have a weak-ish hand, with at least a 5-card suit.

(With a strong hand remember, you would enter the proceedings with an Unassuming Cue-bid.)

LHO opens with 1D; partner overcalls 1S, and RHO bids 2D. You hold:

(a) ♠ K75	(b) ♠ 863	(c) ♠ –
♥ QJ964	♥ AKJ63	♥ KQJ9874
♦ 542	♦ 7	♦ 765
♣ Q3	♣ 9742	♣ 642

(a) 2S. Do not show your hearts. Partner does not want to hear about them, and you are happy to support spades and have them led.

(b) 2H. You could support partner's spades, but you would far rather have a heart led, so that you can return a spade to partner. If partner passes 2H, you will not be upset.

(c) 2H. If partner re-bids 2S, you are quite happy to re-bid 3H.

Jump Overcall
These bids, at the 2-level or higher, can be played to show different values. In modern Acol, they show hands of inter-mediate strength, the requirements being as follows:

(i)   A high quality 6-card suit, or longer.

(ii) At the 2-level, 11–15pts at the 3-level, 12–16pts.

Unlike a Simple Overcall, this bid is a two-edged sword. If partner holds anything at all to help you, you will probably be making the contract, whilst if he holds a poor hand, you will still have barraged your opponents safely.

Careful attention should be paid to your vulnerability. If, in making a Jump Overcall, you have to bid at the 3-level, you should make sure that you match the top end of the above requirements when the vulnerability is adverse.

Responding to a Jump Overcall is straightforward, and requires an even strong adherence to the "support or shut-up" rule. As partner has promised a 6-card suit, you require only 2-card support to raise.

Unassuming Cue-bids are only rarely used in response to a Jump Overcall, because the level is that much higher. In general, as the Jump Overcall has been an effective barrage in itself, you will only raise partner when you see a Game contract in the making, rather than as a further barrage.

Pre-emptive Overcall

This is an overcall at the third available level, and shows a similar hand to the pre-emptive opening bid. To clarify the different overcalls:

1H, <u>1S</u>	is a Simple Overcall, as is	1H, <u>2C</u>
1H, <u>2S</u>	is Jump Overcall, as is	1H, <u>3C</u>
1H, <u>3S</u>	is a Pre-emptive Overcall, as is	1H, <u>4C</u>

The Pre-emptive Overcall requires:

(i) a 7-card suit, or longer, and

(ii) fewer than 10pts.

Particular care should be taken when vulnerable, as this is a high-risk, high-gain bid.

Your RHO opens 1C, and you hold:

♠ KQJ9876   When non-vulnerable, this hand demands a clear-
♥ 72   cut 3S overcall. If your opponents have a heart fit,
♦ 4   they will have to guess it at the 4-level. Notice the
♣ 974   high quality suit, and the absence of values outside
             it. If vulnerable, 1S is probably enough.

Responding to a Pre-emptive Overcall is exactly the same as responding to an opening pre-empt. (See page 65.)

Once again, it is important to remember that the pre-empt will already have caused your opponents considerable discomfort by using up their bidding space. It is, therefore, largely unnecessary to continue the barrage.

1NT Overcall
This is the one overcall which definitely shows a strong hand, for which you require:

(i)   16–18pts, and a reasonably balanced hand, and
(ii) two stoppers in the suit the opponent has opened.

This latter point is one which is often forgotten in the excitement of holding all these points, but is usually remembered once your opponents have led their suit, and start running off lots of tricks in it...

You require two stoppers because this is the suit likely to be led, so one stopper will be used immediately, and a second one will be required when, as is likely, you lose the lead subsequently whilst establishing your own long suit.

Your RHO opens 1D, and you hold:

♠ Q43   This is a text-book example of a 1NT overcall, a
♥ AQ6   balanced hand with 17pts, and two stoppers in
♦ AQ93   your opponents' diamond suit. Still, if partner
♣ K54   holds little, you will have your work cut out.

What should you bid over an opponent's 1D bid on this hand?

♠ J5   At first sight 3C seems best, but count your
♥ Q53   tricks. 1NT will make very quickly on the likely
♦ A3   diamond lead, whereas 3C will need help from
♣ AKQJ53   partner. You only require one diamond stop
                as your long suit is already established, and
yielding six tricks without effort. So overcall 1NT. Your poor
hearts and spades are not a problem – if partner has nothing,
the opponents may double you, but you can retreat into 2C.

With a long <u>solid</u> suit, you require only one stopper
in your opponents' suit to overcall 1NT.

Responding to a 1NT overcall follows the same format as responding to an <u>opening</u> bid of 1NT, but as the overcall guarantees a range four points higher than the opening bid, all the responses require four points fewer. (See page 28 for the chart of responses to 1NT.)

Notice that Stayman should be played opposite a 1NT overcall, although you need to agree this with partner before playing.

Unusual NT Overcall
This conventional bid should be discussed beforehand with partner, but I would expect most competent players to be playing it automatically.

Whenever an overcall of NTs is not a natural bid, it is deemed to be "Unusual" The three natural NT overcalls are: an overcall of 1NT; an overcall of 2NT in the protective position (see page 170); 3NT over an opening pre-empt.

All other NT overcalls are "Unusual NT Overcalls".

This bid shows a minimum of 5–5 distribution in the two lowest-ranking un-bid suits, and asks partner to Show Preference between them.

The bid is made less on point count, more on quality of suits, but if you and your partner wish to lay down minimum and maximum points counts for it, do.

Imagine that RHO opens 1S, and you hold:

♠ 4	On this hand you should overcall 2NT. This
♥ 74	shows a minimum of 5–5 in the lowest-ranking
♦ KQJ98	un-bid suits. If your LHO passes, partner must
♣ AJ1098	now Show Preference between your two suits.

If he actually likes one of your suits, and holds a good point count, say 10pts+, he may choose to jump in your suit, in the same way as in response to a Take-Out Double, as I will be explaining in the next section.

If you have already passed, an overcall of 1NT would be Unusual. After all, you can scarcely be holding 16–18pts.

In this example, you are the dealer, and you pass. Your LHO bids 1H, your partner passes, and your RHO bids 1S:

♠ –	The best way to compete is with an Unusual
♥ 852	NT Overcall. Having passed, you can bid 1NT,
♦ QJ987	which should now be taken as Unusual. If your
♣ KQJ98	LHO now passes, your partner should Show
	Preference between your minor suits.

The Unusual NT Overcall can be used up to any level – except the 7-level. (It would be difficult for partner to Show Preference for one of your suits at the 8-level…)

On this hand, LHO opens 1H, partner passes, and RHO bids 4H. You hold:

♠ 86	A bid of 4NT would be an Unusual NT Overcall
♥ –	showing at least 5–5 in the two lowest-ranking
♦ KQJ86	un-bid suits. Partner must now choose one at the
♣ AQJ987	5-level. Notice the suit quality, and the extra
	distribution (6–5) for use at this high level.

If your opponents have bid two suits, the Unusual NT still shows 5–5 or better in the un-bid suits. As you could also double to make partner bid (see page 107), I suggest that you keep the Unusual NT Overcall for weaker hands, but those with good intermediates in your 5–5 suits.

LHO opens 1D, partner passes, RHO responds 1S, and you hold:

♠ 6   This is perfect for an Unusual 2NT Overcall.
♥ QJ1098   Notice again, the suit quality. If the opener
♦ 54   passes, your partner must Show Preference
♣ KQJ43   between your suits. Of course, if the opener
             does re-bid, then your partner need not bid if
             he does not like your suits.

Opposite an Unusual NT Overcall, you must keep awake, and be of an unselfish nature.

LHO opens 1S, partner bids 2NT, RHO passes, and you hold:

♠ 9532   Tempting as it may be to bid hearts, you must not.
♥ AKJ63   Partner holds 5–5 in the minors, and wants you to
♦ 4   choose between them. A simple bid of 3C will
♣ J64   suffice – and at least you know you have an 8-card
             trump fit.

Finally, remember that this useful Unusual NT Overcall tells your partner a great deal, but it will also help your opponents if they end up playing the hand, as they will have a clear idea as to the distribution of the outstanding cards. Reserve this bid, therefore, for hands where your suit quality is of a very high standard.

A close relation of the Unusual No-Trump Overcall is a gadget called "Michaels Cue-bids", which also shows a 5–5 or longer hand, this time anchoring to the major suits. See page 118 for more details.

OVERCALLS

SIMPLE OVERCALL

A high quality 5-card suit, or longer, probably with three of the five honours including Ace or King, and
At the 1-level: 8pts – around 15pts
At the 2-level: 11pts – around 16pts.

JUMP OVERCALL (intermediate strength)

A high quality 6-card suit, or longer, and
At the 2-level: 11pts – around 15pts
At the 3-level: 12pts – around 16pts.

PRE-EMPTIVE OVERCALL

A high quality 7-card suit, or longer, and
Fewer than 10pts – best used when non-vulnerable.

1NT OVERCALL

Reasonably balanced hand, 16–18pts, two stops in opponents' suit. Possibly, long minor suit, and one stop in opponents' suit. With 18pts+, double, then re-bid NTs. (See page 115.)

UNUSUAL NT

At least 5–5 distribution in two lowest-ranking un-bid suits. Partner must Show Preference if next opponent passes.

Doubles: Take-Out or Penalty?

The question of whether partner's double is for Take-Out or Penalties is one that occurs frequently at the table, and is the cause of many bridge "discussions" – usually in plaintive falsettos or oozing hubris – which continue long past the last of the cucumber sandwiches...

Let's clear it up.

Firstly, you must be clear as to the difference between the two terms.

A Take-Out Double is intended to make partner bid his best suit, at a suitable level, with a view to the Doubler's side playing the contract.

A Penalty Double is intended to penalize the opponents, who may have strayed too high in the bidding, or whose trump suit may be splitting badly. On these, the Doubler's partner is normally expected to pass.

You may be relieved to hear that even the very top players often grind to a halt after a double, because sometimes the Doubler's intention is far from clear.

However, for all but those involved at an expert level of the game, there are simple guidelines to remember to avoid disasters:

Your double is for PENALTIES
if partner has made a positive bid of any kind.

A double over an opening bid of 1NT
is always for PENALTIES.

Otherwise, your double is for TAKE-OUT if there are still at least two un-bid suits, and your partner has not made a positive bid (he can have passed, several times). You can double even if you have previously passed yourself.

Obviously, however, whenever your opponents bid slowly up to the 4-level or above, with both you and partner passing quietly, and one of you suddenly doubles, this is going to be for penalties.

At lower levels, remember the above rules and, if in doubt, assume the double is for Take-Out.

Incidentally, don't make a Penalty Double if you think your opponents might go one off. The odds are not in your favour. They stand to gain much more if they make than you will if they go one down.

For example, if you double your opponents in 4H when they are not vulnerable, and they *do* go one down, you will score 100pts instead of 50 – a gain of 50pts.

If they make 4H doubled, they will gain an extra 120pts, plus another 50pts for the insult. That makes a total gain for them of 170pts. So the odds are against you if you double for one down.

Double on distribution, not points, and only when you think that they will go *two or more* down.

Established partnerships may play a "Negative Double" system, but although the bid itself is simple, the affect it has on your overall bidding is quite significant. Attempt these bids only if you play with a regular partner or group of players who all agree to play this addition to the system.

Take-Out Double
This is the other positive action which you can take after an opponent's opening bid. Unlike some of the overcalls you have seen, it is a genuine attempt to buy the contract for your side. As the name suggests, when you double your opponents, you are actually asking your partner to take you out into his best suit.

You will not make this bid, however, just because you hold a few points. You require **all** the following features to make a Take-Out Double:

(i)   At least 12pts if you have not already passed. (You cannot have too many points for a Take-Out Double.)

   If you have passed already, the bid will then be understood to rely more on distribution than point count, but partner will still expect 9–11pts.

And

(ii) A shortage (void, singleton or doubleton) in your opponent's suit, or one of them if there are two.

And

(iii) A choice of suits. If your opponents have bid only one suit, you guarantee at least three cards in each of the remaining suits.

   If your opponents have bid two suits, you promise at least 4–4 distribution in the remaining two suits.

   Also, if your opponent bids one major suit and you double, you are promising four cards in the other major suit.

Your RHO deals, and opens 1H:

(a) ♠ K873   (b) ♠ KQ98   (c) ♠ Q76
     ♥ 3   ♥ 63   ♥ 4
     ♦ AQ54   ♦ AQ86   ♦ AQJ85
     ♣ QJ98   ♣ K93   ♣ K532

(a) A perfect text-book Take-Out Double.

(b) Not quite so pretty, but still ideal for this double.

(c) Unsuitable for a Take-Out Double, as you hold only three cards in the other major. A 2D Simple Overcall is probably the best action with which to begin.

The Take-Out Double is equally useful when your opponents have bid two suits. It now shows at least 4–4 distribution in the remaining two suits. It also asks partner to choose between them.

LHO opens 1S; partner passes; RHO bids 2D.
You can double on each of these hands:

(a)	♠ A32	(b)	♠ 5	(c)	♠ 98
	♥ KQJ8		♥ QJ987		♥ 9762
	♦ A3		♦ 87		♦ A5
	♣ KQ98		♣ AKQ95		♣ AKQJ8

You may also double having passed. Partner will expect around 10pts, and the usual distribution.

You deal and pass. LHO opens 1H; partner passes; RHO bids 2C. You can double on each of these hands:

(a)	♠ KQ63	(b)	♠ QJ954	(c)	♠ KJ98
	♥ 2		♥ 8		♥ –
	♦ AQ976		♦ AK532		♦ KQ862
	♣ 985		♣ 98		♣ 5432

There is one other position in which you can make a Take-Out Double, although it is often forgotten.

This is the **Re-Opening Double**.

Imagine that you open the bidding with 1S, LHO overcalls 2H, and there are then two passes back to you. You hold:

♠ AJ853 You should double. Once again, this shows a
♥ 7 shortage in the suit your opponent has bid, and a
♦ KQ87 choice of remaining suits. Partner should deduce
♣ AJ8 that you hold five spades as, with two 4-card suits,
you would have opened the lower ranking one.
Partner can now return you to 2S or, if he prefers, either of your other suits; he can bid safely at the 3-level, knowing you hold support. This bid does not show more than a couple of extra points over a bare opening bid, and is much more informative than re-bidding 2S or even 3D, both of which would be poor bids.

Notice that the key to each of these examples is the short-age in the suit or suits bid by the opposition, coupled with the choice of suits offered by you.

Responding to a Take-Out Double

Knowing when to double is not too difficult. It is the responses which seem to cause trouble to many players. This is mainly because most text-books teach a series of point counts for the responder to remember.

As we have seen, reaching the right contract, especially a suit contract, has very little to do with points, and much more to do with finding a good fit. When responding to a Take-Out Double, this is exactly how you should be thinking.

Firstly, you must be clear on whether you have to respond to a Take-Out Double or not.

Imagine that LHO opens 1H, and your partner doubles. If RHO passes, it is essential that you make a bid, however weak you are. Why?

If you were to pass, because you held a poor hand or happened to hold a few hearts, the opener would probably pass too, and the contract would be 1H doubled, which he would make. You may not think this too bad, and indeed it wouldn't be; they would score 60 below instead of 30, and 50 above for the insult. What would hurt are the likely doubled overtricks: non-vulnerable they score 100 each, vulnerable, 200 each.

So, imagine they are vulnerable, you have passed your part-ner's double, and your opponents make their contract with three overtricks – as they might well. You have now given away 60 below the line, and 650 above the line. This is almost the equivalent of their making a small slam. So don't be surprised if your partner gives you an old-fashioned look when you tell him that you were "too weak to bid".

The weaker you are, the more important it is that you do take your partner out of his Take-Out Double.

In short, if your partner doubles, and the next opponent passes, <u>you have to bid</u>.

The only conceivable hand on which you could pass is a strong hand, with excellent strength and length in your opponent's suit. Having such a hand is most unlikely, so it is easier just to remember that <u>you have to bid</u>.

Everything changes if RHO bids. Now, there is no need to bid if you hold a poor hand. By bidding, your opponent has taken your partner out of his double for you. Of course, if you hold a hand on which you would like to bid, then you should still do so.

If RHO redoubles, then there is a special technique for bidding. (See Bidding after a Redouble, page 124.)

Having understood when you have to bid, the most important thing to remember now is that partner has told you almost everything about his hand when he doubled, so the rest is up to you.

When you hear your partner double, you should imagine that he holds a 4-4-4-1 shaped hand (the singleton in the opponent's suit obviously), and 13pts. This may not be exactly what he holds, but it should be about right. Then remember that:

In response to partner's Take-Out Double, you must bid as many of your best suit as you think you can jointly make.

LHO has opened 1H, partner doubles, and RHO passes. What should you respond on these hands?

(a) ♠ 5432   (b) ♠ KJ98   (c) ♠ J7   (d) ♠ Q7642
     ♥ 86432   ♥ 8532   ♥ 963   ♥ A854
     ♦ J9   ♦ A5   ♦ KQJ86   ♦ AQ8
     ♣ 54   ♣ J73   ♣ K83   ♣ 5

(a) 1S. You have to bid, so show your best suit confidently.

(b) 2S. This time you are much happier. With a known 4–4 fit in spades, and a presumed minimum of 22 HCP between you, eight tricks is a reasonable target.

(c) 3D. If partner is 4-4-4-1 with 13pts, as you should be imagining, then nine tricks, with diamonds as trumps, seems about right. If partner is much better, he can bid on.

(d) 4S. You have an opening hand opposite an opening hand. Partner holds four spades so you have a fit. As partner is short in hearts, and you are short in clubs, the tricks will roll in.

Above all, remember that, other than bidding at the lowest available level – which may mean you have nothing as in example (a) – you must bid as many of your best suit as you think you can make opposite partner's hand.

There is the flip side to this as well, of course.

RHO opens 1H, you double, LHO passes, and your partner bids 2S. What should you bid now?

♠ AQJ7   It looks obvious to bid on. But wait a moment.
♥ 6   Partner has bid as many of his best suit as he
♦ K742   thinks he can make if you hold 13pts and are 4-4-
♣ QJ98   4-1. As that is exactly what you have, you must
           pass. Only if you hold extra points, say 16pts,
should you consider bidding on. Most often you will just pass whatever partner responds to your double.

UNASSUMING CUE-BID

LHO opens 1D, your partner doubles, RHO passes, and you hold:

♠ AJ76 You want to bid Game, but you don't know in
♥ AJ76 which suit. It would be very sad to bid 4H, and
♦ A54   then find that partner only holds 3-card support
♣ 83   there, but 4- or 5-card spade support. Or, to guess
        wrong with the cards the other way around. The
solution is to bid 2D. This Unassuming Cue-bid asks partner
to describe his hand further, and suggests that you have
roughly equal holdings in both major suits. (With a minor and
a major suit to choose between, you would always opt for the
major.) All partner does now is name which major he prefers,
and you will raise him to Game.

You might use this Unassuming Cue-bid without so many
points, just wanting to decide in which part score to play. All
you require is enough points to play in whatever partner
responds.
    What if partner passes 2D? Then he is not paying the slight-
est attention. Try a sharp kick to prevent a re-occurrence...

A bid of the opponents' suit always asks partner to describe
his hand further, one way or another.
    Here is an example of a sequence using the Unassuming
Cue-bid in response to a Take-Out Double, incorporating one
further feature:

West	East	N	E	S	W
♠ Q6532	♠ KJ87	–	–	1D	DBL
♥ AQ8	♥ KJ65	NB	2D	NB	3S
♦ 4	♦ 653	NB	4S	NB	NB
♣ AKJ6	♣ 82				

East used the Unassuming Cue-bid planning to play in 2H or
2S. However, West chose spades and jumped to 3S. This
showed extra points and distribution. Had he merely bid 2S,
East would have passed, and the excellent Game contract
would have been missed.

The Unassuming Cue-bid can be used when both opponents have been bidding:

West	East	N	E	S	W
♠ KJ3	♠ A742	–	–	1D	DBL
♥ KQ93	♥ A876	2D	3D	NB	3H
♦ 4	♦ 653	NB	4H	NB	NB
♣ A6543	♣ KJ				

All that happens is that the Unassuming Cue-bid occurs one
level higher than before. If North had bid 3D, East could have
bid 4D, asking partner to choose a major suit.

In other words, you can use an Unassuming Cue-bid at any
level, provided you are strong enough to stand whatever
response partner will make.

RESPONDING NTs

Responding to a Take-Out Double with a NT bid is not what
partner wants to hear. His strength lies in his shortage in the
opponents' suit, and his support for everything else. By responding in NTs, you deny 4-card majors, and confirm that the only
suit in your hand worth bidding is your opponents' suit.

Once again, you should imagine that partner holds 13pts
and 4-4-4-1 shape, and bid as high a contract as you think you
can make between you. The point counts you need are basically the same as for the NT responses to a suit opening bid
(see page 34), but in this case a bid should promise two stoppers in the opponents' suit.

LHO opens 1D, partner doubles, and RHO passes. You
hold:

(a) ♠ KJ6	(b) ♠ J42	(c) ♠ KQ65
♥ 753	♥ Q	♥ Q54
♦ KJ63	♦ AQ3	♦ Q74
♣ J74	♣ KJ7642	♣ A32

(a) 1NT. Stoppers in diamonds, and no other suit to bid.

(b) 3NT. You might try 5C but, as usual with a long minor suit, NTs should be in the forefront of your mind. Don't worry about your poor major suit holdings. Partner has good cards in those suits. And you must bid Game: you hold an opening hand opposite an opening hand.

(c) 4S. Partner wants to hear your major suit. 3NT might be right, but the lack of a decent diamond stopper should stop you from even considering it.

Doubler's Re-bid
There are two, rare, occasions when you would make a Take-Out Double with hands which don't conform to the usual requirements. These involve doubling, and then bidding on over partner's likely weak response. They are both very strong manoeuvres.

1. Double, and then change suit.

RHO opens 1H, and you hold:

♠ AKQJ98   You might bid 4S, but this could confuse
♥ A5   partner as the bid usually denotes a Pre-empt.
♦ AQ4   You are too strong for a Jump Overcall, so the
♣ 63   correct way to show the strength of your hand
            is to double and then bid spades over what-
            ever partner bids.

Changing suit after partner has responded to a double denies the usual 4-4-4-1 style hand, and shows a very strong hand. The requirements are somewhat fluid, but a minimum hand would contain a very high quality 5-card suit, more often a 6-card suit, with a total of 7½ Playing Tricks, or more, in your own hand. Points? You need about 17 as a minimum.

The bid is not forcing, but very highly invitational. With as little as 3-card trump support and an outside King, partner should think of raising. With two possible tricks, he should bid Game immediately.

2. Double, and then re-bid NTs.

RHO opens 1D, and you hold:

♠ A65   You are too strong to overcall 1NT, which would
♥ K5   show 16–18pts. (See page 101.) So you should
♦ AQ5   double, and then re-bid NTs at the lowest avail-
♣ AKJ54 able level. This shows 19–21pts, possibly 22pts,

and allows partner to pass or raise accordingly. With over 22pts you can jump to the next level.

Penalty Double of 1NT
A double of 1NT has traditionally been played as penalty oriented, asking partner to decide whether to risk it for penalties, or pull you into his best suit if he feels he is not strong enough to beat 1NT.

Many experts now feel that a double of 1NT should <u>always</u> be meant for penalties, and I recommend that you adopt this policy with partner, regardless of whether your opponents are playing a Strong or a Weak NT.

With balanced hands, you should hold a minimum of 16 good points (plenty of intermediates, or a 5-card suit) over a Weak NT, and at least 18pts over a strong NT. Occasionally, when your partner is very weak, your opponents will make 1NT doubled but, in the long run, you will find that playing the double of 1NT as a mandatory Penalty Double will gain many hundreds of points.

You can double 1NT on distributional hands too, with no restriction on points. When you are on lead, it will be the tricks you can take which will be important. At Duplicate

Pairs especially, you will find your results improving dramatically on hands like these, when RHO opens 1NT:

♠ Q2 Your first thought might be to bid 2H, or even
♥ AKQJ84 3H, but to make these you would need tricks
♦ A53 from partner. On lead against 1NT doubled,
♣ 74 you are certain to get a plus score. Do not worry
about missing a Game contract – if partner
holds the extra tricks required for Game, imagine the enormous penalty you will extract against 1NT doubled.

This type of distributional double of 1NT is likely to be less successful after 1NT – Pass – Pass (fourth-in-hand), because partner may not lead your long suit, and it is just possible that the opposition can run off 7 tricks before you gain the lead. With the above hand, I think I would still double and take my chances, however, rather than bid my suit.

Double of a Pre-empt
There are many different actions that you can take after an opening Pre-empt by an opponent, and you should agree your choice with partner at the beginning of the session. The most widely played, however, is merely an extension of the standard Take-Out Double. The requirements are the same, although making your partner bid over, say, a 3S Pre-empt, you should be a couple of points stronger, especially when vulnerable. A minimum of 14 HCP would be worth keeping in mind.

The one opportunity you have lost on the basis of this agreement, is of doubling your opponents for penalties. The only solution, when holding a good hand for a Penalty Double, is to pass smoothly, and hope that partner can make a Take-Out Double. If he can, you pass with a clear conscience, and take a big penalty.

RHO opens 3D. You hold:

(a) ♠ KQ65   (b) ♠ KQJ987 (c) ♠ A43   (d) ♠ Q532
     ♥ QJ75   ♥ A43   ♥ A5   ♥ AKQ4
     ♦ 8   ♦ 64   ♦ KJ6   ♦ 754
     ♣ AQ43   ♣ A3   ♣ AKQ53   ♣ Q2

(a) A perfect Take-Out Double in this position.

(b) 3S. Unsuitable for double, with a one-suited hand.

(c) 3NT. Good diamonds, and the long minor suit, should suggest NTs.

(d) Pass. You are short of points, not short in diamonds, and hold nothing in clubs. A Take-Out Double would be horrible.

Incidentally, there is no such thing as an "optional double" of a Pre-empt, although you will hear people suggesting just such a system. Take-Out Doubles intrinsically offer partner the option of passing. That option, as we have discussed, occurs far more rarely than most people think. To encourage your partner to take that "option" is just asking for trouble!

Immediate Cue-bid
An immediate cue-bid of your opponent's suit (1H, 2H) used to be played as Game-forcing, showing the kind of hand on which you would have opened 2C. Because this scenario is so rare, most players use it to show a two-suited hand. The most common agreement is to use **Michaels Cue-Bids**.

An immediate cue-bid of your opponent's suit shows 5-5 or longer in the two major suits, about 10pts or more, and good quality in the suits shown. If the next opponent passes, your partner must show preference, by choosing between your two major suits, even if he only holds two or three card support.

If your opponent opens a major suit, the Michaels Cue-Bid shows 5-5 in the other major suit and one of the minor suits. If partner cannot play in the major suit, he responds with a conventional 2NT bid and this asks the Michaels Cue-Bidder to name his minor suit, in which the partnership will now play.

Responding After an Intervening Take-Out Double

When your partner opens the bidding, and the next opponent then doubles, your available responses are different and wider-ranging than if the opponent had passed.

Let's run through your various options one by one:

I PASS

The most common mistake inexperienced players make is to panic when their partner has been doubled, and attempt to make an erroneous "rescue" of partner, conceding a large penalty unnecessarily, plaintively claiming that "I had to take you out of the double, partner".

Remember that it is the <u>Doubler's</u> partner who must take his partner out of the double, not you, so you should be quite happy to pass on the hands that you would normally pass on, namely those with fewer than 6pts.

The so-called "Trap Pass" is when you choose to pass on stronger hands. Because the Doubler's partner will have to bid if you pass, it is sometimes a good idea to do this, and await developments. You will get another chance to bid. It is possible that your opponents will bid too high, and that you will be able to double them for penalties. This will not work against good players, but you can probably extract a couple of bid penalties off your friends until they work out that they need to improve their bidding...

If you pass, and your opponents don't bid too high, you will have to remember to bid up on the next round otherwise partner will think that you hold very few points.

II REDOUBLE

This bid is played in a myriad of different ways, and you should discuss them with your regular partner(s).

A Redouble technically says "we are so certain that we are going to make this contract, even though the opponents have doubled, that we are prepared to double the stakes once again, with all the extra points at risk which that entails".

However, things are not as simple as that, and a Redouble ought really to be looked at quite differently.

For general use, I would recommend that, in short, Redouble means, "Get your finger on the doubling trigger partner."

In more detail, it is saying, "Partner I hold at least 10pts so, as you have opened, I know that this hand belongs to us. However, I am probably short in your suit (fewer than 3 cards), so doubling our opponents may get us richer than bidding on ourselves. I want you to double the opponents if they bid any suit in which you hold good cards, and I will do the same.

"If you can't double them, I promise to make at least one further bid, so don't re-bid your suit unless you are happy to have it as trumps without any support from me. If I do support your suit later, then I have 3-card support and a good hand."

The advantage of a Redouble over a Trap Pass is that it informs your partner that you have a good hand, and allows either of you to double your opponents for penalties.

It does, of course, warn your opponents to keep the bidding low, but informing your partner should be your priority.

Your partner opens 1H, your RHO doubles, and you hold:

♠ KJ95   This is perfect for Redouble. You do not want to
♥ 5   play in hearts, and any contract the opponents name
♦ AJ74   should fail. Your Redouble has requested that
♣ QJ98   partner should either double or keep quiet, so get
            ready to double your opponents on the next round.

III SUPPORT PARTNER'S SUIT

Because the Doubler is wanting his partner to choose one of the remaining suits, you should do everything possible to use up their bidding space if you can support your partner. For this reason, with 4-card support or more you should, after an intervening Take-Out Double, raise one level higher than if there had been a pass.

Partner opens 1H, RHO doubles, and you hold 4-card heart support:

If you were going to pass, you should now bid 2H.
If you were going to bid 2H, you now bid 3H.
If you were going to bid 3H or more, you now bid 2NT.

This last bid is not a natural bid of NTs, but a conventional bid, telling partner that you have at least 10pts and 4-card support for his suit. If the next opponent passes, as is likely, partner <u>must</u> now bid at least 3H (straight to 4H if he would have raised 3H to 4H in the normal course of events), and then you can bid on or pass accordingly. He is not permitted to pass your 2NT bid if the next opponent has passed.

This may seem unnecessarily complex, but it allows immediate raises in partner's suit to be used as a pre-emptive action, which is a useful tactic after a Take-Out Double.

Your partner opens 1H, your RHO doubles, and you hold:

(a) ♠ 543   (b) ♠ KJ6   (c) ♠ A4
    ♥ 8642   ♥ K962   ♥ KQ86
    ♦ K9642   ♦ 52   ♦ K752
    ♣ 7   ♣ J975   ♣ 743

(a) You would normally have passed, but now pre-empt with 2H.

(b) You were going to bid 2H, so now jump to 3H.

(c) Bid 2NT, telling partner that you would have bid <u>at least</u> 3H without the intervening Take-Out Double. If your LHO passes, partner will bid 3H with a minimum opening, or 4H with extra points.

IV 1NT

An informative little bid, played in a similar way to usual (see page 32). However, after the intervening double, do not respond 1NT with a singleton or void in partner's suit, trying to rescue him – it won't work. Just pass and expect your opponents to bid on. If you do respond 1NT, this promises two or three card support for partner's suit and 6-9pts. Now, partner can judge whether to bid on later in the auction.

V CHANGE OF SUIT

After an intervening Take-Out Double, most players agree that a change of suit is natural and forcing as usual, and that it shows tolerance (a doubleton honour or three card support) for partner's suit. It is important still to show a 4-card major suit at the 1-level if you have one, since your side may still hold an 8-card major suit fit.

Partner opens 1H, RHO doubles, and you hold:

♠ KJ75	Although the doubler is likely to hold four spades,
♥ J8	your partnership could still hold an 8-card spade
♦ A543	fit. Also, if your partner holds a strong balanced
♣ 754	hand he may be pleased to know that you hold four spades to allow him to make his planned re-bid of no-trumps.

VI JUMP SHIFT

This bid is normally the first move towards a slam (see page 129), but after an intervening Take-Out Double it is simply used as Game-forcing showing an opening hand or stronger, and a high quality 6-card suit. (You might have an extra good 5-card suit.) Partner supports, or continues to show the shape of his hand, until a Game contract is reached.

If your partner opens 1NT and is doubled, this is intended for Penalties, not Take-Out. (See page 116.) It is therefore vital that you make a Weak Take-Out bid (see page 18) as usual, on the basis that you are likely to be safer with a 5-card suit as trumps, than with partner playing in 1NT doubled.

If you are very weak (say, 3pts or fewer) you should make a Weak Take-Out with only a 4-card suit, as it is essential that you attempt to de-fuse a very nasty situation. Such a rescue may only result in a similar large penalty against your side but, equally, it may be enough to persuade your opponents to continue bidding, rather than doubling you again. Above all, bid confidently...

Bidding After a Redouble

Here is the last position affected by a Take-Out Double, one with which most players seem to be unfamiliar. Let's set the scene.

You are West, dealer North, and the bidding has run as below:

♠ 542	N	E	S	W
♥ 9753	1H	Dbl	Rdl	?
♦ 9				
♣ J6532				

Your first instinct may be to pass quickly. After all, partner has another bid, and you have a rotten hand. However, would you be happy if partner bids 2D, and is then doubled? Then, you might rather wish that you had been in clubs where, as partner has doubled, showing a minimum of 3-card support for all the un-bid suits, you know you have at least an 8-card fit.

Bidding after a Redouble does not show any points, because it should be obvious to everybody that you are weak. Why?

North has an opening hand, East doubled, showing about 13pts, South redoubled showing a minimum of 10pts, so there aren't many left for you. If you do bid after a Redouble it is to ensure that your side reach the safest contract at the lowest available level, so that if you are doubled the penalty will be as small as possible.

So, in the example above, you should have bid 2C. This tells partner one special thing: that you hold <u>two</u> more cards in the club suit, than in any of the other suits he might bid. (Remember, he has promised to hold all the un-bid suits – spades, diamonds, and clubs.)

The bid does not promise any points, or any length. Just two more cards in clubs, than in spades or diamonds.

And, once more for good measure, *it does not promise any points*. If you do pass after a Redouble, all you are telling partner is that you have no clear preference for any one of the possible suits, and that you are content to let him choose the suit in which you play.

This is a complicated, but logical, area of bidding. If you are trying to improve your bridge, it is worth studying it with your partner.

Let's take a look at a couple of further examples with the same bidding sequence:

♠ 8742	N	E	S	W
♥ 96432	1H	Dbl	Rdl	?
♦ K3				
♣ Q9				

Here, you should bid 1S. You learnt that your partner holds 4-card support for the other major when he doubled, so you have a 4-4 fit. Your opponents will probably bid on to a part score, and may even reach 4H, at which point you will be well placed to defeat them. If you pass, partner may bid 2C or 2D, which will be uncomfortable, and possibly doubled.

♠ 854   You are pretty unhappy about the whole sorry
♥ 9532   business, but here you must pass and let partner
♦ J75   decide what low-level contract he wants to be in.
♣ Q64   You don't really care what he chooses.

Above all, remember that you must never let 1H redoubled become the final contract. If you do, the declarer makes Game for making only seven tricks, and gets very, very rich on the redoubled overtricks. So, if you pass, and the opener passes (as he probably will), partner MUST bid something.

By way of example, assume that your vulnerable opponent plays in 1H Redoubled, and makes nine tricks.

He makes Game, scoring 120pts below the line for 1H Redoubled ($30 \times 2 \times 2 = 120$), plus 800pts above the line for the two redoubled vulnerable overtricks ($400 \times 2 = 800$), and a further 100pts above the line for making a redoubled contract.

This amounts to more than he would score for a vulnerable small slam. Christmas has arrived early for your opponents...

TAKE-OUT DOUBLES

Note: a double of an opening 1NT is always for Penalties.

Otherwise, if partner has not made a positive bid (he can have passed, even several times), and there is still a choice of suits available, then, if you double, it is for Take-Out. You can double even if you have previously passed yourself.

If partner has made a positive bid of any kind, then your double is for *Penalties*.

A Take-Out Double shows:
12pts+ (on a previously passed hand, 9–12pts)
AND a shortage in your opponents' suit(s)
AND a minimum of 3-card support for all un-bid suits.

(If opponents have bid 2 suits, you promise a minimum of 4-4 in the other 2 suits. If they have bid one major suit you promise at least 4 cards in the other major.)

Partner assumes you hold 13pts, and 4-4-4-1 shape, and bids as many of his best suit as he thinks he can make.
   Having doubled, you always pass, unless a) you hold extra points (in which case you may raise accordingly), or b) partner asks you to re-bid, by using an Unassuming Cue-bid.

An Unassuming Cue-bid (bidding the opponents' suit) asks you to choose which major suit you prefer. Partner normally uses it when he has similar length in both majors.

A NT response to a Take-Out Double shows:

two stoppers in the opponents' suit, and denies major suits.
Point counts match responses to opening bids.
Rarely, a Take-Out Double may show:

(a) a balanced hand with 19+pts.
   The Doubler re-bids NTs with 19–22pts   : at the lowest level
   with 23+pts   : at a jump level

Or

(b) a strong single-suited hand (usually 6-cards +) of 7½+ tricks. The Doubler re-bids in his suit at lowest available level. Even with a single trick, responder should then raise him.

ACTION AFTER AN INTERVENING TAKE-OUT DOUBLE

Partner opens the bidding with one of a suit, the next opponent makes a Take-Out Double, and you must find a bid:

PASS

Usually 0–5pts.
Might be a "Trap Pass" with a good hand, waiting for opponents to over-bid before doubling them – only advisable against weak opposition.

REDOUBLE

10pts+, and usually less than 3-card support for partner. Suggests to partner that doubling your opposition may be better than bidding on, and asks him not to re-bid his suit.
   Subsequent support of partner's suit shows 3-card support, and 10pts+.

SUPPORT
PARTNER

Assuming the sequence 1H – Dbl – ?
with 4-card trump support, raise partner one level higher than if there had been no double.
   If you were planning to bid 3H or more, respond 2NT. This conventional bid tells partner to re-bid 3H if holding a minimum – you can pass or bid on – or 4H if maximum.

1NT

Balanced hand. 6–9pts, promising 2 or 3-card support for partner's suit.

CHANGE
OF SUIT

6–10pts, natural and forcing.
   With stronger hands, you should Redouble or Jump Shift.

JUMP SHIFT

12pts+, forcing to Game, high quality 6-card suit.

10

SLAM BIDDING

Jump Shift

The Jump Shift response to a suit opening, so called because of the *jump* in level, and the *shift* in suit, is greatly over-used and misused, and must be reserved for hands with <u>slam</u> potential.

If your partner opens the bidding and you hold an opening hand, there is no need to jump. A simple change of suit is forcing, and the auction to Game can be developed slowly.

Before using a Jump Shift you must believe that there is a good chance of slam, <u>and know in which denomination you are going to play</u>. If you do not know which suit will be trumps, there can be little point in wasting valuable bidding space by jumping.

Take these examples. Partner has opened 1H, and you hold:

(a)   ♠ AJ853   (b)   ♠ A64
       ♥ Q4   ♥ 3
       ♦ QJ86   ♦ AKQJ
       ♣ KJ   ♣ KJ732

(a)   Game is your only realistic target at the moment and you don't know which suit you'll play that in. 1S forces partner to re-bid, and with that extra information you can decide how to proceed.

(b) Despite 18 HCP, it would be very unwise to Jump Shift in response to 1H, as you have no idea in which suit you are going to play. Just respond 2C, hear partner's re-bid, and proceed from there.

Fourth Suit Forcing (see page 57), and a new suit at the 3-level, are both forcing measures for the next round if you are still not sure where you're going. With a misfit, Game may well be your limit.

The requirements for a Jump Shift are as follows:

a strong hand, usually 16pts or more but sometimes just a very good distributional fit, and either

very good support for partner's suit,
or
a self-supporting suit of your own, in which you will be happy to play even if partner holds a small singleton.

You Jump Shift, and then partner has to make his planned re-bid, whether it be NTs, a second suit, or a simple re-bid, at one level higher than he expected, due to your jump.

Your re-bid now tells partner on what your Jump Shift was based:

If you Jump Shift, and then <u>support</u> partner with your re-bid, he knows that your Jump Shift was based on good support for his suit. You will also be promising that the suit into which you jump-shifted is headed by at least the Ace or King, but you are no longer promising length in that suit.

If you Jump Shift into a suit, and then re-bid that suit, partner will know that you hold a self-supporting suit.

Either way, whatever suit the Jump Shifter <u>re-bids</u> sets the trump suit. There is no argument.

West	East	_W_	_E_
♠ A6	♠ KQJ42	1H	2S
♥ AJ743	♥ KQ965	3D	3H
♦ KJ86	♦ 54	etc	etc
♣ 84	♣ A		

East Jump Shifts because of his excellent shape and trump support for partner. West makes his natural re-bid of diamonds, one level higher than he expected and, when East supports hearts with his re-bid, the suit is set and slam enquiries can get underway as explained shortly.

West	East	_W_	_E_
♠ 63	♠ AKQJ942	1C	2S
♥ AJ4	♥ K5	2NT	3S
♦ K82	♦ A4	etc	etc
♣ AQJ42	♣ 53		

East Jump Shifts as he holds a hand on which he would have opened 2S. West's re-bid of 2NT shows 15–16pts and his balanced hand (it is the lowest re-bid of NTs he can now make), and East's 3S confirms that spades will definitely be trumps. A spade slam can now be reached using Blackwood or Cue-bidding. (See pages 132 and 139.)

So, a Jump Shift is forcing to Game, and highly invitational to a slam.

When used properly it allows you to establish a trump fit, in a slam-going situation, at a low enough level to allow plenty of subsequent investigation to reach the right final contract.

The days of a Jump Shift being made just because you hold 16pts are long gone, thank goodness. Simply remember the main requirements:

You must think that there is a slam on <u>and</u> know in which suit it is going to be played. Now, the jump makes sense.

Blackwood Convention

These are straightforward conventional bids asking partner to show how many Aces or Kings his hand contains. The convention is often used before bidding to a slam contract.

Once a suit has been agreed – or you, yourself, have decided the trump suit and that you have enough combined values on which to bid a slam – you should use this convention to check the number of Aces and Kings your partner holds.

A bid of 4NT asks partner how many Aces his hand contains. The responses, harking back to the suit order of rank, are simple:

5C = 0 Ace or All 4 Aces
5D = 1 Ace
5H = 2 Aces
5S = 3 Aces

There should be no confusion between 0 Ace and 4 Aces. The bidding prior to Blackwood will make misunderstanding impossible. (There is a 16pts difference between 0 and 4 Aces!)

If you and your partner have all four Aces between you, and only if you do, you can then ask partner how many Kings he holds. 5NT does this via the following responses:

6C   = 0 King
6D   = 1 King
6H   = 2 Kings
6S   = 3 Kings
6NT = 4 Kings

Basically, you will only ask for Kings if you are hunting for a Gram Slam, as often the response to 5NT will take you past a safe 6-level contract.

For example, you should exercise extreme care when clubs is your trump suit. You may require two Kings to make 7C a reasonable contract, but when your partner responds 6D to show only one King, you will have passed the sensible spot of 6C.

Try to anticipate partner's response, and check that you can cope with whatever he says. If you cannot, you may do better to settle for a safe Game contract instead.

All that seems pretty straightforward. There are, however, three essential rules to which you must adhere to avoid disasters:

1. If you initiate Blackwood you must know in which denomination the final contract will be played, otherwise you will find yourself at a very high level with an impossible decision to make.

2. A player initiating Blackwood must not hold a void in his hand. If he does, he may not be sure whether partner holds the right Ace.

   You hold this hand, and your partner has opened 1S:

♠ KQ87   The correct bid would be a Jump Shift to 3C and
♥ –   then support spades. Incorrectly, however, you
♦ A642   bid 4NT straightaway. Partner responds 5D,
♣ KQJ87   showing one Ace, and now you do not know
whether he holds the vital A♣, or the useless A♥. Cue-bidding would solve this problem. (See page 139.)

3. Before going ahead you must hold first or second round control (Ace, King, or singleton) in every suit, or have great expectation of the partnership having such control. Otherwise, you may hold three Aces and three Kings between you in the same suits, and still lose the first two or three tricks because the other suit is unguarded in both hands.

You hold this hand, and your partner has opened 2S:

♠ K43   Your hand is tremendous, but bidding 4NT now
♥ 65   would be reckless. If partner responded 5H,
♦ KQJ76   showing two Aces, you would not know whether
♣ A54   you had two quick heart losers in a slam contract.

          You should first respond 3S – the strongest response available – and then hope that partner can initiate Blackwood, or that a Cue-bidding sequence sorts out that worry in the heart suit.

Whilst you would not initiate Blackwood with a void in your hand, it may be that your partner bids 4NT and that you, as responder, are looking at a void. How should you treat it?

Firstly, if it is in a suit which your partner has bid, you should ignore it altogether. It is more likely a hindrance than a help.

Also, if you are short in trumps in the agreed suit, the void will not be much use, so again ignore it and give the usual Blackwood response.

If, however, you believe that the void will be an asset to partner's hand, you are able to show it using a simple manoeuvre. Work out the correct Blackwood response for the number of Aces your hand contains, and then make this response at the 6-level, rather than the 5-level.

For example, your partner opens 2S, you bid 3S, and partner bids 4NT:

♠ KJ76   You have excellent trump support, and
♥ A543   diamonds have not been bid, so your void is an
♦ –   asset. Usually, you would respond 5H, to show
♣ AJ762   two Aces, but now you can bid 6H which shows
               two Aces, and a working void.

Before making such a bid, do check that the response will not embarrass partner by taking him past a safe level. In the above example, 6S is almost certain after the 2S opening bid, and 7S must be likely. The response of 6H therefore is unlikely to worry partner.

ROMAN KEY-CARD BLACKWOOD

This modern version of Blackwood is gaining in popularity, particularly amongst Duplicate bridge players. Its significant advantage is that the responses include information about the King and Queen of trumps – both vital cards when slam hunting. Here is an abridged version of simple RKCB.

A bid of 4NT asks partner to name how many of the FIVE key cards he holds. The five key cards are the four Aces and the King of the agreed trump suit. If no trump suit has been clearly agreed then, for the purposes of RKCB, the last naturally bid suit is assumed to be trumps. At the end of the auction, the 4NT RKCB bidder must bid the correct contract.

The responses to 4NT are as follows:

5C = 0 or 3 key cards
5D = 1 or 4 key cards
5H = 2 key cards and no trump Queen
5S = 2 key cards plus the trump Queen

There should be no confusion between zero or three key cards, nor between one or four, since the bidding before using 4NT should reveal partner's strength.

5H and 5S both show two key cards – the most likely response, but also add information about whether the Queen of trumps is held.

If all five key cards are held between the partnership and you wish to investigate for a Grand Slam, the 4NT bidder can use 5NT to ask for Kings. In RKCB, however, the responder does not show how many Kings he holds, but instead bids the suit (or suits) in which he holds a King (not including the trump King which was included as one of the five key cards in the initial response to 4NT).

With more than one King, responder bids the lowest-ranking suit first and, if the 5NT bidder signs off in the agreed suit, if the responder holds a second King, he can now show it by bidding that suit also.

In the full system, you can also ask for the trump Queen after the 5C and 5D responses. However, this simple version is a useful first step towards adopting RKCB into your system. Before playing, check with new partners as to which version of Blackwood they would like to play.

DIRECT KING BLACKWOOD

This complicated sounding bid is in fact nothing more than a logical approach to one aspect of Acol.

As the responses in the sequences 2H – 4H and 2S – 4S deny any Aces (see page 86), it would be illogical for 4NT to ask how many Aces partner held. Therefore, after these sequences, <u>and only these sequences,</u> a bid of 4NT by the opener asks directly for Kings; hence comes the name Direct King Blackwood.

4NT Opening
This is a very rare opening bid indeed, because of the strength and shape required, but one worth a quick mention as this bid is <u>not</u> Blackwood.

A 4NT opening bid asks partner to name the suit in which he holds an Ace. The responses are as follows:

5C = I hold no Aces
5D = I hold A♦
5H = I hold A♥
5S = I hold A♠
5NT = I hold two Aces
6C = I hold A♣

Such an opening bid would only be made on a hand where you are interested in just one or two specific cards for a Grand Slam. This is a classic example:

♠ AKQJ1098
♥ –
♦ A
♣ KQJ109

6S is obviously making whatever partner holds, but 7S relies on A♣. No other card is remotely important. If partner responds 6C or 5NT to the 4NT opening you can bid 7S; over anything else, you will settle for 6S.

Quantitative Bidding

This is another bid of 4NT which is <u>not</u> Blackwood.

A direct response of 4NT to an opening bid of 1NT or 2NT is not asking for Aces, but is Quantitative. This is because a NT contract is decided mostly by points, so sometimes it is necessary to find out partner's exact point count. The process works on the assumption that you require a combined point count of 33 or 34 pts to make 6NT a reasonable prospect. (See page 6.)

1NT – 4NT and 2NT – 4NT each ask partner to pass if he holds minimum points for his opening bids, but jump to 6NT if he has maximum points.

You would bid 1NT – 4NT holding 19 or 20pts. Opposite 12pts in partner's hand, you would hold a combined 31 or 32pts – plenty for 4NT, but not enough for 6NT. Opposite 14pts in partner's hand, the combined total would be 33 or 34pts, and partner will bid 6NT.

You would bid 2NT – 4NT holding 11 or 12pts. Similar arithmetic applies. Partner will bid 6NT if he has 22pts.

If partner holds 13pts for his 1NT bid, or 21pts for his 2NT bid, he must study the "texture" of his hand. If it contains plenty of 10s and 9s, or a 5-card suit, then he should treat it as having maximum strength and jump to 6NT. With poor intermediates, he should treat it as of minimum strength and pass.

1NT or 2NT – 5NT is a rare Quantitative Raise, which I do not really recommend as there is a slight danger you will reach 7NT missing an Ace! However, should your partner make this bid...

A 5NT response asks you to bid 6NT with a minimum opener, and 7NT with a maximum opener. A good 23–24pts are required opposite 1NT, and a good 14–16pts opposite a 2NT opening.

There are other quantitative bids, and positions in which you can play NT raises as quantitative, but these are the most common, and the only ones within the scope of this book.

Grand Slam Force (GSF)

Another rare bid which you may choose to discuss with your partner. It is certainly not in general use in social bridge games, or in most Rubber bridge clubs.

The bid of 5NT, <u>when not preceded by 4NT</u>, asks partner how many of the top three honours he holds in the agreed suit. The responses are stepped as with Blackwood:

6C = I hold None of the top three honours
6D = I hold One of the top three honours
6H = I hold Two of the top three honours

and with All Three of the top three honours, you bid the Grand Slam.

As with Blackwood, care should be taken when approaching a minor suit slam, as partner's response may take you past a safe level.

Some pairs resolve that when the agreed suit is clubs, they will revert to the old "Josephine" GSF, in which 5NT instead asks partner to bid 6C unless he holds two of the top three honours in which case he can bid 7C.

N.B. This is definitely an area for discussion with a regular partner or group of players. You should not assume a casual partner knows anything of the Grand Slam Force.

Disasters at the slam level are one of the prime causes of partnership disharmony. If you are faced with what you think is the right bid, but you are worried that your partner won't understand it, just swallow your pride and make the less adventurous, simple bid instead.

Sometimes bridge becomes an "anything-for-a-quiet-life" game. If you desire to play fast and loose the whole time, take up poker...

Cue-bidding

You should use Blackwood when you are merely interested in HOW MANY Aces and Kings your partner holds, but employ Cue-bidding when you need to know WHICH Aces and Kings partner holds.

Take this hand for example:

♠ AK8642   You open 1S, partner responds 3S. Your hand
♥ A65   is difficult to assess now. If partner's high cards
♦ KQ52   are in the right places, you will be making 6S,
♣ –   even 7S. If they are misplaced, 4S may be the
              limit.

There can be no point in using Blackwood because, if partner announces that he holds one Ace, you won't know whether it is the vital A♦, or the useless A♣. (A♣ would be useless, because you have no club losers anyway.)

What is needed on this type of hand is a system whereby partner can pinpoint where his high cards lie, without taking the bidding too high. It is for this purpose that Cue-bidding is so invaluable.

*Unless you have a close partnership understanding,
Cue-bidding should only commence when you and your partner
have agreed a suit, in a strong sequence.*

For example, in each of the following sequences the trump suit has been quite definitely agreed:

1S – <u>3S</u>   2H – <u>3H</u>   2C – 2D   1S – 2D
                                           3C – <u>4C</u>   2H – <u>4H</u>

If the opener were to mention another suit now, it could not possibly be a natural bid of that suit. What would be the point, when you have already agreed your trump suit?

And if the opener were interested only in Game, he would just bid it, or pass if Game had already been reached. So, if he now bids another suit, it must have a different meaning. That meaning is that he is heading for a slam contract, and it is known as a Cue-bid.

A basic Cue-bid announces to partner that you hold "first round control" (a feature that can control the suit the first time it is led, namely, an Ace or a void) in the suit that you mention. As well as showing partner where you hold first round control, it asks him to name the suit or suits where he holds controls, so that you can both build up an accurate picture of where the high cards lie in one another's hands.

The most worrying element of Cue-bidding for inexperienced players is the concern that they will make a Cue-bid, and their partner will suddenly pass, leaving them in a suit where they are void, or hold only the Ace. Playing with a partner who is awake, this cannot happen. You will only Cue-bid after you have definitely agreed trumps and, therefore, even if your partner doesn't know what is going on, he will be able to return you to the agreed suit.

Indeed, it is <u>part</u> of Cue-bidding that if at any time you cannot, or do not wish, to proceed further, you just return to the agreed suit as a sign-off.

The other important element is that you always show your controls in the cheapest available order. This means that if you miss out a suit, your partner can deduce that you do not hold an Ace or void in that suit.

Seeing examples of Cue-bidding is much easier than all this theory:

West	East	West	East
♠ AKQ942	♠ J853	2S	3S
♥ AK5	♥ 873	4C	4D
♦ KQ52	♦ AJ	6S	
♣ –	♣ KJ84		

West opens 2S, and receives a positive 3S response. West's 4C bid suggests to partner that they should investigate a slam, and that he holds A♣ or void. East is then required to announce where he holds an Ace or void, and the 4D bid shows A♦ or void in diamonds. This is just what West wants to hear, so he now jumps to 6S.

This is just a simple Cue-bidding sequence, but it raises several very important points:

1. West could not use Blackwood as his hand contains a void. If he had bid 4NT, East would have shown one Ace, and West would not have known whether it was the vital A♦, or the useless A♣.

2. When West started to Cue-bid, he bid the cheapest control first, namely 4C. If he had bid 4H, he would have wasted bidding space, and denied holding controls in the cheaper suits – clubs and diamonds.

3. Had East held A♣, he would have known that his partner held a void in the suit. As it was he did not know whether 4C showed A♣ or a void. This didn't matter; he just co-operated by bidding 4D, showing his A♦.

4. Had East held no Aces or voids, he could have signed-off by returning to 4S. However, if this were the case, he should have responded 4S immediately.

By now, you may have realized that it is impossible to show the Ace of trumps in a Cue-bidding sequence because, if you return to the agreed trump suit, it is a sign-off manoeuvre. For this reason, you can assume that the player who starts Cue-bidding should hold the Ace of trumps. However, there is no reason why you can't Cue-bid to find out the position of a particular card, and then revert to Blackwood to check the total number of Aces and Kings in the hand.

This is one of the key advantages of Cue-bidding – the ability to find out whether a slam is even worth investigating – and still keep the bidding below Game level.

Just as important as reaching good slam contracts is staying out of bad slams.

West	East	West	East
♠ AQ987	♠ KJ42	1S	3S
♥ KQ3	♥ A8	4D	4H
♦ AKQ	♦ J85	4S	NB
♣ 54	♣ QJ76		

After the 1S – 3S agreement, West Cue-bids 4D, which denies a control in clubs, as a 4C bid would have been cheaper and he would therefore have bid this first. East co-operates by Cue-bidding his A♥. West, still concerned about his two club losers, signs-off in 4S. If East holds A♣, he should start up the bidding again by bidding 5C, and a slam will be reached. As it is, the slam-try has resulted in E/W staying out of an unmakable 6S.

This sequence provides a difficult but logical inference which East will do well to take:

When West signs-off in 4S, East may be worried that there is still a slam on if West holds K♣ or a singleton club. However, he can have neither of those holdings because, if he had, he would have used Blackwood, either to begin with, or over the 4H Cue-bid. The reason he has not used Blackwood is because he is holding two or three small clubs, and has remembered that you require first or second round control in every suit to use Blackwood. (See page 133.)

So far, you have seen Cue-bidding sequences which just show Aces and voids. As you become more confident, you can Cue-bid Kings and singletons (the second round controls) as well. But remember:

As with Blackwood, you should only be interested in Kings once you have established that you hold first round control in every suit.

To see how sequences can develop, look at this example:

West	East	West	East
♠ –	♠ K742	2H	3H
♥ AK65432	♥ Q98	3S	4C
♦ AQJ2	♦ K7	4D	4S
♣ K6	♣ A984	5C	5D
		7H	

West opens a maximum 2H, and East gives a positive 3H response. 3S, 4C, and 4D are all Cue-bids showing first round controls. East is permitted to assume that West holds the Ace of trumps, as he started Cue-bidding, and therefore all the suits are controlled.

East's excellent hand is worth another move, so he now shows his second round controls. 4S shows K♠.

This card is of no interest to West opposite his void, but as 6H looks a fine contract anyway, he can afford a little more investigation. The card he really wants to hear about is K♦. West Cue-bids 5C, showing K♣, and is then delighted to hear 5D from East, which shows K♦. Now, with first and second round controls in every suit, West can bid the Grand Slam with considerable confidence.

If West had wanted to check whether his partner held the Queen of trumps he could have used the Grand Slam Force after East's 5D (see page 138), a convention often used after a Cue-bidding sequence when a 7-level contract is in the offing. As it was, even if East did not hold Q♥, the Grand Slam was very likely to make.

That example demonstrated how easy it was to show all the vital cards required for a Grand Slam. In "real life", bidding rarely runs as smoothly as that but, when it does, it is enormously satisfying. Sometimes, however, the bidding grinds to a halt almost as soon as it has begun.

West	East	West	East
♠ AKQJ987	♠ 5432	2C	2D
♥ AKQ	♥ J8	2S	3S
♦ 643	♦ 985	4C	4S
♣ –	♣ AJ76	NB	

Having agreed spades, East is probably thinking that he holds a very good hand considering he showed a weak hand with his 2D response. However, things go rapidly downhill when West Cue-bids 4C. As East holds A♣, West's bid must be showing a void, and so A♣ is not nearly as valuable. With no other control of any kind to show, East signs-off in 4S. If West were to continue Cue-bidding, then East could show his A♣, but West, wisely on this hand, passes before getting too high.

So remember:

If at any time you have nothing further to Cue-bid, you should sign-off by returning to the agreed trump suit. This does not necessarily conclude the auction. Partner can continue Cue-bidding if he has the strength and further controls to show.

Finally, it is also worth reminding yourself that, after weak suit agreements:

1C – 2C   1D – 2D   1H – 2H   1S – 2S

if opener re-bids a new suit, it will be a Trial Bid, hunting for a possible Game contract (see page 46). Cue-bids occur only after a *strong* suit agreement.

Advanced Cue-bids
These are Cue-bids made before an actual suit agreement, but made in such a way as to make your fit with partner's suit obvious.

There are a great many different types of these bids, but in this book, concern yourself with just one type, which occurs after an opening bid of 1NT or 2NT.

After the sequence 1NT – 3H, there are only two re-bids the opener can make: 3NT, if he holds only two hearts; and 4H if he holds three hearts or more. There are no other bids the 1NT opener can make. (See page 21.)

What then, do you suppose is the meaning of this sequence?

1NT – 3H
<u>4C</u>

It cannot possibly mean that the opener has a long suit of clubs. (Having opened 1NT you are never allowed to proffer information about your suits unless asked.)

What it shows is that your opening hand contains the following elements:

(i)   4-card heart support.

(ii) A maximum (14pts) hand, probably with a doubleton somewhere.

(iii) A♣ (but not A♠, or you would have Cue-bid 3S).

In other words, you are saying, just in case partner is thinking of a slam "I have the perfect hand, and here is a Cue-bid on the way to bidding 4H".

If partner has no interest in a slam, he will re-bid 4H, and there the matter ends – you've just slipped in a piece of information below Game level.

If he is interested, he can now continue to Cue-bid, launch into Blackwood, or bid the slam immediately.

The beauty of this Advanced Cue-bid is that it will always occur beneath the level of a Game contract. Therefore, it is free information, which can be acted upon or ignored by partner without pushing up the level.

Here is an example of this sequence in action:

West	East	West	East
♠ KQJ9	♠ A8753	1NT	3S
♥ A98	♥ 6	4C	4D
♦ 32	♦ A4	4H	6S
♣ A542	♣ KQJ76		

West's 4C Advanced Cue-bid agrees spades, shows a maximum 14 points hand, and A♣. East, who would have had to be brave to bid on over a simple 4S re-bid, now co-operates with the Cue-bidding sequence, and can bid 6S with confidence.

In fact, 7S would be a good contract, but you have done very well to bid the small slam with only a combined 28 HCP count.

Alternatively:

West	East	West	East
♠ AKQ	♠ 872	2NT	3H
♥ KQ83	♥ AJ742	3S	4H
♦ KQJ4	♦ 982	NB	
♣ J4	♣ Q6		

Here, East is not the least bit interested in a slam, even when encouraged by a maximum strength partner – he just signs-off in Game. Notice that, once again, the Advanced Cue-bid has been slipped in beneath the level of Game.

The opener can make an Advanced Cue-bid after the sequences 1NT – 3C/D or 2NT – 3D but, as these responses are mild slam tries, the responder is far more likely to co-operate anyway.

What about 2NT – 3C? Well, that's Stayman or, as you will see, Modified Baron... (See page 150.)

11

CONVENTIONS

Several conventional bids are part of, or have passed into, the Acol System – the Strong 2C Opening, for example. When you say that you play Acol, your partner will assume that you play them.

Stayman and Blackwood are two other bare essentials which you really must play. After that, it's up to you; but if you are reckoning to become a reasonable social player, I would recommend that Fourth Suit Forcing, Trial Bids, the Unusual NT, and Cue-bidding are all part of your artillery.

If I were playing with the same partner for a whole session, as opposed to switching partners after each rubber (or Chicago – another popular form of scoring for the social game), I would briefly discuss Unassuming Cue-bids, and the two extra conventions which I describe in this section – Modified Baron and Asptro.

There are, beyond the scope of this book, literally hundreds of conventions which you can opt to play and, if you are forming a regular partnership, then it is a good idea to experiment with many of them. Keep your favourites and chuck out the rest. For the most part, however, social players, and club Rubber bridge players keep conventions to a minimum. Some clubs ban all but the most basic ones from everyday play. For this reason, I am restricting this chapter to just two extra bids.

I recommend <u>Modified Baron</u>, which is an excellent addition to an Acol-based system, and also <u>Asptro</u>, a counterbid (or defence), when your opponents open 1NT. Asptro has limited use for Rubber bridge or Chicago players, but it is extremely useful for Duplicate bridge players, since to disturb your opponents' 1NT contract is an excellent tactic at that form of scoring.

Modified Baron

This convention is sometimes called "5-card Stayman". The truth is that it is a mixture of 5-card Stayman and the old Baron Convention. As you will see, it carries several advantages over straightforward Stayman.

As 2H and 2S openings nowadays promise 6-card suits, it is often more convenient to open 2NT when you have a strong hand containing a 5-card major suit. In the past, the danger of opening 2NT with a 5-card major was that a 5-3 fit in the major suit was missed.

Modified Baron replaces Stayman opposite a 2NT opening, as it checks for both a 4-4 <u>and</u> a 5-3 fit in the majors.

The bid may also be used after the sequence, 2C – 2D – 2NT, which shows a balanced hand of 23/24pts.

REQUIREMENTS:

Apart from prior arrangement with partner, the Modified Baron response requires only enough points to make Game a possibility (about 4pts is usually the minimum). It should be used on EVERY HAND CONTAINING A 3- OR 4-CARD MAJOR. However, if the hand also contains a 5-card major or longer, that suit should be bid in preference to using this convention.

<u>The response which starts the convention operating is 3C.</u>

RESPONSES:

The responses to this 3C bid are very simple.

3H/3S	says that your hand does contain FIVE cards in that suit.
3D	denies 5-card major, but shows at least one 4-card major.
3NT	denies even a 4-card major suit.

After a 3D response, the convention now takes on its Baron form:

> If the 3C bidder holds no 4-card major, he settles for 3NT, or, with 13pts+, heads for a NT slam.
> With one or both 4-card majors, the 3C bidder now shows his major suit (hearts first if holding both), and the opener then bids his.
> If, at any time, a 4-4 fit is found, the 3C bidder either raises Game, or heads for slam – the decision being entirely his.

If it becomes evident that a 4-4 fit does not exist, either player returns to 3NT. The 3C bid is forcing to Game, and may be the prelude to a slam. As the opener has made a Limit Bid, this is a decision which must be left to the responder.

West	*East*	*West*	*East*
♠ KQ987	♠ A42	2NT	3C
♥ KQ3	♥ J642	3S	4S
♦ A3	♦ J852	NB	
♣ A42	♣ 76		

East is happy to explore for either a 3-5 spade fit, or a 4-4 heart fit. In response to East's 3C bid, West shows his 5-card spade suit, and the superior 4S Game is thus reached easily.

West	East	West	East
♠ Q987	♠ KJ42	2NT	3C
♥ KQ3	♥ AJ84	3D	3H
♦ A3	♦ 85	3S	4S
♣ AKQ4	♣ 762	NB	

After the Modified Baron response, West bids 3D, which denies a 5-card major, but promises at least one 4-card major. East bids his lower major first; it does not match with West's suit, so West bids his 4-card major. This matches up with East for a 4-4 fit, and Game is bid.

Asptro

This is quite a complicated convention. It needs to be discussed and practised with a partner before play. In order to explain the gadget fully, it would be necessary to produce many examples. This section therefore serves merely as an introduction to the convention.

The Asptro convention is used only as a counteraction to an opening 1NT bid.

The reason why the Weak NT is now so widely played is that it is pre-emptive by nature, and that makes it difficult for you, as the opposition, to compete.

With a single-suited hand, especially a minor, you should, and can afford to, be content to try to defeat 1NT. For this reason the overcalls of 2C and 2D have been used for the Asptro Convention against 1NT, for those times when you want to intervene with 2-suited hands, on which it *is* a good idea to get involved in the bidding.

REQUIREMENTS:

Different point counts can be agreed for this gadget but, in general, I would recommend about 10–14pts. With greater distribution, such as 6-5 or 6-6, you might enter the auction with fewer high card points.

With 16pts, or more, even with a long suit, your first thought should be to double 1NT for penalties. (See page 116.)

Your points should be concentrated in your two suits, rather than outside, and the suits should contain good intermediates.

Over a 1NT opening, an overcall of:

2C shows HEARTS & ANOTHER suit – at least 5-4 distribution.

2D shows SPADES & ANOTHER suit – at least 5-4 distribution.

Note: The major suit does not need to contain five cards; it may only be the 4-card suit.

If you hold a spade/heart two-suiter, you should anchor to the shorter major when deciding which overcall to make.

RESPONSES:

Partner's responses are quite complicated, but hopefully logical. They are based on the desire to find a decent fit to ensure that you make your contract or fail only by one trick (making your result superior to allowing your opponents to succeed in 1NT). You may occasionally miss a Game contract, but that is only a small price to pay for disrupting your opponents as often as possible.

The three responses shown are the ones that you will use ninety-nine per cent of the time. Because they are quite detailed, the remaining responses (which you are unlikely to require) have been omitted.

1. With 0-10pts, holding four cards or more in partner's major suit, bid 2 of that major suit. Partner will always pass unless he holds five cards in the suit and is completely maximum for his Asptro bid.

   If you hold an opening hand or stronger with 4-card support or better for partner's major suit, consider jumping to the 3-level in partner's suit, or going directly to Game. Remember that your partner may hold as few as 10pts for his bid.

2. With up to 12/13pts, holding 3-card support for partner's major suit, and a singleton or void elsewhere in the hand, bid 2 of the major suit.

   You do this because you suspect that your partner's other suit is the one in which you are very short and, even a 4-3 fit will play adequately at the 2-level. However, you do not wish to move to higher level.

3. Without 3-card support for partner's major suit, or if you have 3-card support but no singleton or void elsewhere, bid the suit above the one your partner has used. This is a relay bid, asking partner to describe his hand further.

   If he holds five cards in his major suit, he will rebid it. If you are satisfied with this, because you hold a doubleton or 3-card support, just pass. If you are not satisfied, bid 2NT. This asks partner to name his other suit, and there you will play.

   If he does not hold a 5-card major suit, over your relay bid, he will show his 5-card suit and you will almost certainly pass that bid.

These responses will allow you to find an 8-card major suit fit when it exists, to play in 5-2 major suit fit or a 4-3 fit when that is correct to do so. Otherwise, it will guide you to play in partner's other suit when that is the superior action.

Let's take a look at some examples of the convention in action:

South opens 1NT:

West	East	West	East
♠ QJ987	♠ 104	2D	2H
♥ 985	♥ QJ32	2S	NB
♦ 3	♦ AJ85		
♣ AKQJ	♣ 762		

West's 2D shows spades and another suit. East's 2H denies 4-card spade support, or 3-card spade support with a marked shortage elsewhere in his hand. West's 2S confirms that he holds a 5-card spade suit, and East is happy to pass this.

South opens 1NT:

West	East	West	East
♠ A6543	♠ 2	2C	2H
♥ KQJ8	♥ 1076	NB	
♦ 654	♦ KQ72		
♣ 8	♣ A7532		

West remembers that with both major suits, there is a small advantage to anchoring to the shorter major. He therefore bids 2C, showing hearts and another suit. East, despite holding only 3-card heart support, responds 2H because he suspects that his partner's other suit is the one in which he is short. West passes 2H, which is the best contract available. East's best play will be to trump low spades in hand with his 3-card trump holding, saving West's 4-card heart suit for drawing trumps later.

The Asptro bid is forcing. Partner is not permitted to pass just because he happens to hold five or six cards in a minor suit and little else. A fit almost certainly exists somewhere, and problems will only occur if the rules are not followed. The next example illustrates this.

South opens 1NT:

West	East	West	East
♠ KQ952	♠ –	2D	2H
♥ K32	♥ A864	2S	2NT
♦ 7	♦ 96532	3C	NB
♣ KJ54	♣ A763		

East denies 3-card support for partner's declared major by bidding the suit above the Asptro bid. West re-bids 2S, showing that his 5-card suit is spades, and denying that his second suit is hearts (he would have passed 2H).

East is unprepared to stand 2S, so his bid of 2NT demands that partner shows his second suit. West does so, and 3C becomes the sensible contract. Had East incorrectly passed 2D, that contract might well not have made.

South opens 1NT:

West	East	West	East
♠ KQJ9	♠ A876	2D	3S
♥ 32	♥ A84	4S	NB
♦ 52	♦ Q863		
♣ AK654	♣ Q7		

It is not necessary that your 5-card suit should always be the major. Here, the use of Asptro has allowed your side to reach a 4-4 fit in spades which would have been impossible to find without a conventional counterbid to 1NT.

Notice that West only bids on to 4S after East's invitation as he holds a high quality 13pts, when he might have held only 10pts.

Asptro, like all the other defences (counteractions) to 1NT, will not always get you a good result. When you have a misfit, you will regret not simply trying to defeat 1NT, but it is better to bully your opponents than let them relax and, in the long run, this convention should gain you valuable points.

Asptro should be played after 1NT – pass – pass – as well. You can afford to be a little weaker, as there is less danger of being doubled for penalties by the opener's partner. (See Chapter 12, BALANCING, which comes next.)

If your opponents are playing an old fashioned Strong NT, you and your partner may still agree to play Asptro. You require extra points and distribution (a minimum of 5-5 distribution, and 14 HCP). If you are vulnerable, more care should be taken. As usual the quality of your suits is the most important factor.

12

BALANCING

(Protective Bidding)

The term "Balancing" is the American equivalent of our word(s) "Protection" or "Protective Bidding", but I prefer it as it better suggests what this whole business is about.

There are many different arrangements regarding balancing which you can make with regular partners but, for general use, we will look at the most common ones, and the basis upon which each is invoked.

When should you balance, i.e. protect? The answer is that

You are in the Balancing (or Protective) position
at any time in the auction when an opponent has bid,
and there are then two passes around to you.

There are two main reasons for competing at this stage of the auction, both vital for successful competitive bidding:

1. It may help you to push your opponents' bidding too high, winning you penalty points.
2. You may steal part score contracts where, otherwise, your opponents would have.

There are two different positions in the auction where balancing is the appropriate action:

1 AT LOW LEVELS

Before looking at the balancing position itself, it is as well to take in some background thoughts. Imagine you are West, your RHO opens with 1D, and you hold:

♠ AJ65　You have a good 13pts, but you have no good bid.
♥ AQ2　An overcall would be misleading, and to double,
♦ J742　wrong. With no sensible bid available, you should
♣ J5　　pass and await developments.

So, there are times when you will have to pass on hands of up to 15pts, simply because you have no good bid to make. (With 16 HCP+ a 1NT overcall – page 101 – will come into play.) Equally, when partner passes, bear in mind that he may be strong.

Imagine you are now East and your LHO opens 1D, your partner passes, RHO passes, and you hold:

♠ K32　　Normally, you would consider this hand too weak
♥ KJ543　to make an overcall. However, your opponent's bid
♦ 53　　followed by two passes puts you in the balancing
♣ 987　　position; and this means you should overcall 1H.

The reason why you should bid 1H on this hand is fully explained if you look at both terms for bidding in this position: you should bid to *protect* against partner having a good hand on which he was unable to bid, and because you expect that the points are roughly *balanced* between the two partnerships.

Some arithmetic: opener holds no more than 19pts, or he would have opened at the 2-level. His partner has shown fewer than 6pts by not responding. The maximum your opponents can have therefore is 24pts, leaving your side with a minimum of 16pts. You know for certain then, on the hand above, that your partner holds at least 9pts.

Statistically, it is rather more likely that the opener has about 14 or 15pts, his partner 4 or 5pts, and your partner about 14pts. Probably your partner was unable to bid because he held diamonds, and lacked a high quality 5-card suit for an overcall.

The important thing is that the points for both sides are more or less balanced, and whoever can push the opposition past a safe level will win.

Passing in this balancing position is giving your opponents an easy time. You must instead bully and nag them in the bidding at the 1- and 2-levels. But remember, having pushed them up a couple of levels, leave them to go down; don't continue bidding on yourselves.

To make these balancing decisions on WEAK hands a neat device called the Theory of the Deferred King should <u>always</u> be applied. When you look at the above example again in a moment, you will see how it helps.

Theory of the Deferred King
This convoluted sounding theory is actually a straightforward method of bidding in the balancing position when there have been an opening bid and two passes.

All you do is imagine that your hand contains an extra King which you have borrowed from your partner's hand, and then make whatever bid you would normally make on the hand. The King you borrow is not a specific King; it is just 3pts for you to put in your hand. In this way, you will be bidding on your shape, not points – whereas your partner has the points, but presumably no shape.

The important moment comes when partner responds to your bid. He must remember that he has lent you a "King", and subtract that from his hand before responding. This way you will not get too high.

Let's take the hand we saw earlier above, and put the rule, which is easily mastered, into practice:

South opens 1D, you (West) pass, and North passes:

West	East	West	East
♠ AJ65	♠ K32	NB	1H
♥ AQ2	♥ KJ543	2H	NB
♦ J742	♦ 53		
♣ J5	♣ 987		

East (partner) adds a "King" to his hand, and is thus sufficiently confident to overcall 1H. Whether South attempts to re-bid 2D or not, you can bid 2H. Only 2H though, because you must remember that you have lent your partner a King in order for him to make a bid in the first place, so he could be very weak.

If 2H is passed out, you will make it. If N/S bid 3D, you will probably defeat it. Either way, you have a plus score, instead of letting your opponents score points because of your feebly passing out 1D.

So, in the balancing position, overcalls can be made on much weaker hands, with greater reliance placed on your distribution.

Because this affects all overcalls when made in the balancing position, let's review them generally. Notice that if you add on the 3pts for the deferred King to the following point counts, the totals are very similar to those for an ordinary overcall or double:

An Overcall	At the 1-level might be made on as few as 6pts, and a reasonable quality 5-card suit; whilst at the 2-level, a moderately good 5-card suit and <u>8pts would be the minimum requirements.</u>
Take-Out Double	Will have all the usual shape requirements (see page 126), but perhaps as few as 9pts. Note: double of 1NT – for penalties – must still promise 16pts+, regardless of your being in the balancing position.

1NT Overcall This bid does not invoke the Theory of the Deferred King, because the adjusted point range has already achieved its purpose. The range varies, but it is mostly played to show 11–14pts, and at least one stopper in your opponents' suit. You should agree with your regular partner to play Stayman opposite this. With 15–18pts, you should first double, and then re-bid NTs at the lowest available level.

With 19pts+, see 2NT Overcall below.

As there are so many balancing bids which could be weak, we must have a couple of balancing bids which show STRONG hands. Unlike the weaker hands above, these do not involve the Theory of the Deferred King:

A Jump Overcall Whatever strength you normally play your Jump Overcalls, in the balancing position this is a strong bid, promising a 6-card suit, at least 7 playing tricks, and probably around 15 HCP.

2NT Overcall This is not the Unusual NT (see page 102). It is played as a natural overcall. It shows 19–22pts, and two stoppers in the opponents' suit. You should discuss with a regular partner whether you will play Stayman, or Modified Baron (see page 150), opposite this bid.

1. South opens 1D, North passes:

West	East	West	East
♠ J9873	♠ KQ4	NB	1NT
♥ Q3	♥ A84	2S	NB
♦ 543	♦ QJ82		
♣ AK4	♣ J73		

Despite any pre-emptive advantages, West rightly does not overcall with these terrible spades. When his partner balances with 1NT (11–14pts), he makes a Weak Take-Out into 2S, which East passes.

It is essential that both East and West remember that East is in the balancing position after two passes, and that his 1NT overcall shows 11–14pts, and not the usual 16–18pts.

2. South opens 1H, North passes throughout:

West	East	West	East
♠ Q987	♠ KJ42	NB	DBL
♥ J873	♥ 54	2S	NB
♦ AK4	♦ Q987		
♣ K4	♣ QJ9		

East doubles in the balancing position. West would normally jump to 4S in response to a Take-Out Double, but here, remember, he should subtract a "King" from his hand. He is now borderline between bidding 2S and 3S, but as he is responding to a protective double he should err on the side of caution and bid 2S. If East is much stronger than the minimum 9pts he has promised, he can raise the response. Otherwise, he will just pass, as here.

If N/S bid up to 3H, West should be happy just to defend the contract, which E/W will almost certainly defeat.

3. South opens 1NT, North passes:

West	East	West	East
♠ A9	♠ KJ7642	NB	2S
♥ KQ43	♥ 8	NB	
♦ AJ43	♦ 985		
♣ 854	♣ A76		

When East balances with 2S, West should pass. Chances of Game are very remote. Making plenty of part scores, having balanced on light hands, will more than make up for the odd missed Game (and there won't be very many).

In general, it is best to have modest aspirations after a protective bid of any kind. Certainly, unless you and your partner hold a big fit (9 cards) in one suit, Game is unlikely.

4. South opens 1S, North passes:

West	East	West	East
♠ 87	♠ KJ2	NB	2NT
♥ J32	♥ AQ	3NT	
♦ Q7642	♦ KJ5		
♣ A54	♣ KQJ76		

Remembering that 2NT in the balancing position shows 19–22pts, West can happily raise his partner to Game, unless he has agreed to play Modified Baron (page 150) in which case, he would reply 3C, but the resulting contract will be the same. He should not be tempted to show his diamond suit. Partner is not interested.

It is worth emphasizing once again that, as you can see from these examples, the partner of the player doing the balancing is very conservative about supporting him. If you over-bid opposite a balancing bid, it will only serve to discourage your partner from bidding correctly next time. To make plenty of part scores is much better than to worry about the occasional thin Game missed.

II AT HIGHER LEVELS, AFTER SUIT AGREEMENT

Balancing can occur at almost any level of the bidding, and some of the decisions after complicated sequences are quite difficult.

Here, let's just consider one other position in which you should be very keen to enter the bidding on a weak hand.

The bidding runs as follows, and you are West, holding this hand:

♠ Q8542	N	E	S	W
♥ 3	–	–	1H	NB
♦ KQ9	2H	NB	NB	?
♣ J632				

It looks obvious to pass at this point – but think about all four hands rather than just your own, and you will find that it is right to bid. You correctly passed over the 1H opening, North made the weak raise to 2H, and opener could not even muster a try for Game, so he is hardly stacked with points either.

All this marks your partner with quite a few points – but probably too many hearts to have been able to bid – and this means that you should come in with an overcall of 2S.

Now, let's tackle the questions which might arise from this action.

1. What if I push our opponents into Game?

    Then you are playing against a couple of jokers. They have passed out 2H, so it is hardly likely they will suddenly decide Game is on.

2. What if my partner thinks I have a good hand?

    Partner should recognize the "bid and two passes" situation as the balancing position, and count you for a poor hand. Anyway, if you had such a good hand, why didn't you overcall 1S over 1H?

3. What happens if they bid 3H?

    Partner will pass, however many points he holds, because of the balancing principle – the more he holds, the less you hold. The one time he might bid 3S is if he holds 4- or 5-card spade support.

Having pushed your opponents from a comfortable 2H to an uncomfortable 3H, you should be content to let them play. You are really in a no-lose situation at this point: if they make 3H you have lost nothing; if they go down, you have pushed them too high, and got a plus score off a hand where you would otherwise have seen your opponents earning points.

The only way you can lose is to bid on. That is why you must always agree how you will handle balancing with your partners.

In the example above, the reasons why it is safe to enter the bidding at the 2-level, when you were not strong enough to bid at the 1-level are both of key importance:

1. <u>Both opponents have limited their hand</u> – North has shown 6–9pts, and South has passed North's raise – so there is almost no chance of your being doubled.

2. <u>Your opponents have found a fit</u>. Firstly, this means that their hands are more suited to playing a contract than defending one. Secondly, they will be somewhat miffed that you have disturbed their neat little contract, and will probably bid on in a fit of pique.

Indeed, even before the hand has been passed out, I have known opponents who have bid 1H – 2H turn to the opposition and tell them it's their lead. They are presuming that the others will not enter the auction now. You must explode such a presumption.

Let's take another example. You are West again:

	N	E	S	W
♠ 4				
♥ QJ93	–	–	1S	NB
♦ Q9653	2S	NB	NB	?
♣ AQ2				

The opposition bidding, followed by two passes, once more puts you in the balancing position. Your opponents have found a fit, and limited their hands. You are reasonably safe to enter the auction. A Take-Out Double should be your choice. If your opponents push on to 3S, pass and defend that contract. If they do not, a 3-level contract by your side should not fail by many, and may even make.

What about this hand? You are sitting West:

♠ 2		N	E	S	W
♥ KQ53		–	–	1S	NB
♦ A943		INT	NB	2D	NB
♣ Q987		2S	NB	NB	?

Should you double on this hand? It looks all right but, in this case, the opposition bidding should have warned you off. The key is that they have **not** found a fit.

It may be that they do have an 8-card fit in spades. Equally, they may only have seven trumps, and a misfit – North only Showed Preference when he bid 2S, not support. To make partner bid at the 3-level would be risky. North may be itching to make a Penalty Double of either of the other two suits – and, in any event, you may well defeat 2S.

After all, if N/S do only hold a 7-card spade fit, your partner is looking at five trumps...

So, the key factors for balancing at higher levels are these:
Your opponents must have:

1. Found a genuine fit – not just arrived somewhere after being shown preference.
2. Both limited their hands.

Then it is safe for you to enter the bidding with a shapely hand. If partner is paying attention, he will recognize the balancing factors, and not get over-excited when responding.

Rubber bridge players need to take account of one final factor, the score.

If your opponents have a 60 part score, and their bidding has run 1H – 2H, the situation is not the same at all, because they may be bidding to the score. Their 2H bidder may hold many more than 9pts, and their opener has no need to proceed any higher, however strong his hand. In this position, therefore, it would be very risky indeed to apply these balancing principles. Unless you have your bid in full, you should pass quietly.

At all times, a key mantra for competitive bidding is this:

If your opponents have an 8-card fit in one suit, you will also have an 8-card fit in another suit. So you want to bid.

If your opponents have a misfit, so will you. So, you want to defend.

BALANCING
(Protective Bidding)

You are in the balancing position at any time after your opponents have made a bid or bids, and there are then two passes to you.

For example, at the 1-level 1H – NB – NB – ?

WEAK HANDS

OVERCALL   5-card suit, reasonable quality, and
                  At 1-level, 6pts+
                  At 2-level, 8pts+

DOUBLE   Usual shape requirements for Take-Out
                  (page 126). 9pts+
                  (After a 1NT opening, Penalty Double still shows 16pts+)

1NT OVERCALL   11–14pts
                  At least one stopper in opponents' suit.
                  (With 15–18pts, you should double first, and then re-bid NTs at the lowest available level.)

STRONG HANDS

JUMP OVERCALL   6-card suit. 7 Playing Tricks or more.
                  Around 15pts.

2NT OVERCALL   19–22pts
                  Two stoppers in opponents' suit.

At higher levels
Balance only with shapely hands, using protective overcalls and doubles, and only if your opponents have:

1. Quickly found at least an 8-card fit.
2. Both limited their hands, showing them to be weak.

At Rubber bridge, beware of opponents bidding to part scores.

13

KEY PRINCIPLES OF CARD PLAY

Assuming that you have adopted some, if not all, of the suggestions so far, your bidding will certainly have improved. Playing in more ambitious contracts, you may now find that your card play needs a boost. There are stacks of books which delve into every last detail, but much of this is wasted knowledge, because the need for it occurs so rarely. The key principles of play – those which occur frequently – will get you home, and winning, most of the time. The moment they have become second-nature, both your confidence and your capacity for more complicated plays will grow.

The play of the declarer and that of the defenders are directly linked: whatever the declarer wants to do, the defenders should be trying to stop him. If he has one goal, they should have another. So, putting yourself into the mind of the declarer, in an attempt to anticipate what his plan of action may be, is one of the key steps to a successful defence.

There are however, important differences between the play of the cards in suit contracts, and tactics in NT contracts, so I will deal with each separately.

When bidding, you can just about get away with thinking about only two hands – although I hope, by now, you will have realized how important it is to think of the opponents' hands as well. When it comes to card play, it is essential that you try to build up a picture of all four hands. With effort over a period of time, your card play will then improve immeasurably.

Suit Contracts – The Declarer
What do you do when dummy is laid in front of you?

If you just start playing, then you will find you aren't making many of your contracts. All bridge players, even top internationals, pause when dummy hits baize. They are gathering their thoughts.

Don't worry about making a full plan, trying to anticipate every single trick. Rather, your aim should be to have a clear overview of the problems ahead.

Don't waste time telling partner that his bidding was wrong, and instructing him as to what he should have bid. Regardless of whether you are in a good or bad contract it is your duty to give it the best chance you can.

When dummy is laid down four questions need to be considered:

1. How many losers do I have? (See example below.)

2. How many points are there between my hand and dummy?

3. Have our opponents bid and, if so, what?

4. What do I think about the opening lead?

Your *losers* refers to the number of tricks you will lose in each suit, <u>having drawn trumps</u>. Always count finesses as losers as, that way, you will never be disappointed when the finesse fails. Also, it will encourage you to seek a way of making the contract without relying on taking any finesses, which is the correct technique.

Remember too, that you only count losers in your own hand. For this purpose, dummy does not have any losers.

To see what is meant by counting your losers, let's take the following hand as an example.

You are sitting South, playing in 4S:

♠ K74
♥ KJ6
♦ AJ108
♣ 763

♠ AQJ63
♥ AQ8
♦ KQ
♣ 1042

To assess the number of losers on your hand, look at the <u>shape</u> and high cards in your own hand (South), and the high cards in dummy. So:

There are 3 losers in the club suit.
There are 0 losers in the diamond suit.
There are 0 losers in the heart suit.
There are 0 losers in the spade suit – a total 3 losers.

As you are in a contract of 4S, you can afford to lose three tricks, so all looks well.

When you hold few enough losers to make your contract, you should draw trumps as quickly as possible.

This is because the only way you will lose extra tricks is if your opponents start trumping your winners.

If you have more losers than you can afford you must then, before playing the first card from dummy, set about making a rough plan of campaign to get rid of those losers you cannot afford. Often, when this is the case, you have to delay drawing trumps.

Thankfully, there are only three main ways of doing this.

1. Trumping losers in dummy.

♠ K872   Against your contract of 4S, K♣ is led. You have
♥ AQ5   two diamond losers, and two club losers – one
♦ J9743   too many. The simple way to get rid of one of
♣ 4   these is to trump a club in dummy. So, you win
                the first trick and then draw trumps ensuring
♠ AQJ54   that dummy still has one trump left for that club
♥ K64   ruff. By trumping a low club (both if you have
♦ Q2   the chance) your losers are reduced to few
♣ A62   enough to make the contract.

2. Throwing away losers on dummy's long suit.

♠ K87   Against your contract of 4S, K♣ is led. You have
♥ KQJ95   three club and two diamond losers. Your oppo-
♦ 53   nents are likely to cash the first three club tricks,
♣ 852   after which you can win the next trick. The
                successful line to avoid the diamond losers is to
♠ AQJ952   discard them on dummy's long hearts. So, you
♥ A   should play ♠AQ, A♥, and then cross to dummy
♦ A62   with K♠, and play out the hearts throwing away
♣ 943   your ♦62.

The third method of safely divesting your losers often relies on help from the defenders. We will look at that shortly.

In the meantime, hopefully, you will have found these two examples straightforward. If so, you are approaching the hands correctly. Next, you can move on to the other questions you should ask yourself when dummy appears.

Remember, they are:

2. How many points are there between my hand and dummy?

3. Have the opponents bid, and if so, what?

4. What do I think about the opening lead?

Question 2 asks you to assess your combined total, so that you can work out how many HCPs your opponents hold. This is linked to Question 3: if one opponent has opened 1NT, then you know that 12–14 of the outstanding points lie with that opponent. That may not leave many for his partner. And so, all of a sudden, you have a pretty good idea of where all the high cards lie. It becomes easy, *if you ask yourself the right questions at the right time*.

The answer to Question 4 should add to that information. As explained in the section on defence shortly, if a defender leads a King, it is usually form KQ or KQJ. Making a mental note that he holds those cards may be useful now or later on in the play.

Here is a contract many players would fail to make yet, if you ask yourself those key questions, you should find it easy.

West deals and opens 1C and you, as South, end up in 4S:

♠ K74
♥ KJ6
♦ AJ98
♣ 763

♠ Q2		♠ 1065
♥ 543		♥ 9872
♦ 103		♦ 76542
♣ AKQJ98		♣ 5

♠ AJ983
♥ AQ10
♦ KQ
♣ 1042

A♣ is led. You count your losers: 3 club tricks, and Q♠. As you can only afford to lose three tricks, and you are likely to lose three club tricks straightaway, you at least now know that key to success lies in not losing a trick to Q♠.

Now ask yourself Questions 2 and 3:

How many points are there between your hand and dummy? Answer: 28. This leaves 12pts for the opposition.

Have the opposition bid, and if so, what? Answer: Yes. West opened the bidding with 1C.

Surely West must hold all 12 outstanding points in order to justify his opening the bidding? If you consider this to be so – and you should – then you can place West with Q♠ for certain. Now, you will cash A♠ and K♠, playing for Q♠ to fall – by far your best chance on this hand. A thoughtless declarer tries to finesse through East with J♠, and claims bad luck when it fails.

You know that West holds Q♠, so you can hardly get away with looking surprised when he turns up with it.

Question 4 does not add to your knowledge on this hand. The opening lead of A♣ is obviously top of a sequence, but you already know that West held all the outstanding points once you have paused to think about it.

Sound analysis at the start of every hand of declarer play is vital and, as you become more experienced, you will be able to cover this ground quite quickly. In the meantime, remember that there are no prizes for speed at bridge and, if your opponents try to hurry you, they are doing it for only one reason – they want to stop you giving the hand your best shot. So take no notice. If they become objectionable, then stop playing with them. This is a game of skill, not luck.

3. Suit Establishment

The single most important method of developing tricks in suit contracts is "Suit Establishment". In Example 2 on page 174, you saw how you could use winners in dummy's long suit to discard losing cards from your hand. Suit establishment takes this idea a step further, since you will be using a long suit – not necessarily of high quality – to develop extra tricks in order to fulfil your contract. At its best, this is a piece of bridge magic and, for those unused to these techniques, it should prove revolutionary. We'll work our way through the various elements of suit establishment to build up a picture of the entire technique. Master these plays and you will be a force to be reckoned with whenever you play a suit contract.

By the way, unless you are exceptionally receptive to new concepts, I don't think that you can learn this technique simply by reading about it. I urge you to grab a pack of cards and lay out the examples, following the guidance. Continue doing this until you can honestly say: "Yes, I get this. It's beautiful!" Then, you'll know that you are on your way to succeeding as a declarer.

(a) Identifying a long suit

♠ J1095
♥ K65
♦ KQ8
♣ J63

♠ KQ863
♥ A32
♦ J6
♣ KQ10

South plays in 4S, and West leads Q♥. Count your losers. You have one in each suit. Since there are no shortages in dummy, you cannot ruff any of them. Is there a long suit on which you might throw a loser from hand? Apparently not. Look closely at the diamond suit. You hold two diamonds in your hand and there are three in dummy. That makes it a long suit. Indeed,

any suit which contains more cards in one hand than the other, can be considered a "long suit".

Usually, you will want the suit in dummy to be longer than in your own hand, since it is from your own hand that you will want to discard losers. However, occasionally you can use a long suit in your hand to discard cards from dummy, allowing you to ruff later.

Back to our hand. How can you make 4S?

To succeed, you will have to discard your heart loser on dummy's third diamond. However, you are missing the A♦, and you will have to push out this card before you can claim any diamond winners. This is a simple form of suit establishment. You are setting up winners for yourself by playing the suit (and, in this case, losing a trick – A♦ – in order to set up your other diamonds as winners).

There are two further considerations on this hand:

1. You cannot afford to draw trumps before tackling diamonds because, when you lose to A♠, another heart will be led and then, when you lose to A♦, your opponents will cash their heart winner before you have had a chance to throw it away from your hand. This often happens with suit establishment hands: you have to get going on the establishment before drawing trumps because you do not have time to draw them before your opponents beat your contract.

   This may seem risky but, since you have too many losers to make your contract, you will definitely fail if you don't take positive action. If, while you are trying to establish a suit, an opponent trumps in, you will go down – but you were going down anyway. At least this way you've failed trying to make your contract, rather than merely capitulating.

2. You must ensure that you have a means of access – an entry, or entries – into the hand which contains the long suit you are trying to establish (nearly always in the dummy). Maintaining entries into dummy often proves

crucial to your success. Fail to do it and your contract will be likely to fail also.

So, how to make 4S: Win West's Q♥ lead with A♥ in hand. This preserves dummy's K♥ as an entry to reach the table. Now, lead J♦ from hand. Your opponents may well take their A♦ but, if they do not, follow this with 6♦. This time they will surely win. Whatever they return, you can win, cross to dummy with a heart and then play your K♦. On this card, throw away your low heart from hand. With that loser discarded, you have only three possible losing tricks so you can draw trumps. Your opponents make only their three aces and nothing else.

(b) Ruffing out a long suit

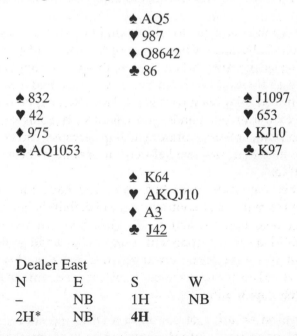

```
                          ♠ AQ5
                          ♥ 987
                          ♦ Q8642
                          ♣ 86

        ♠ 832                              ♠ J1097
        ♥ 42                               ♥ 653
        ♦ 975                              ♦ KJ10
        ♣ AQ1053                           ♣ K97

                          ♠ K64
                          ♥ AKQJ10
                          ♦ A3
                          ♣ J42
```

Dealer East

N	E	S	W
–	NB	1H	NB
2H*	NB	4H	

* with 3-card support for partner's major suit, a weak hand, and a shortage elsewhere, a simple raise is usually the best action.

Here, South plays in 4H against which West shrewdly leads 2♥. This attack on trumps is likely to scupper the simple line of play which would involve you ruffing a club loser in dummy before drawing trumps. Instead, you will have to establish dummy's long suit to provide a discard for at least one club loser. To this end, you will have to attack the diamonds early on in order to push out East's high diamonds. Let's see what you should do.

You win trick one with 10♥ and immediately lay down A♦, followed by 3♦ to dummy's Q♦, which East wins. East is likely to return another trump and, again, you win in hand. Now, cross over to dummy's Q♠ and lead a low diamond. East plays his J♦ and you trump in hand. West also produces a diamond. By the act of ruffing a low diamond in hand, you have extracted all the remaining diamonds from your opponents' hands and left the two remaining diamonds in dummy as the only remaining cards in the suit – and therefore as winners. Finally, draw your opponents' trumps and then cross to dummy's A♠ to enjoy your two diamond winners on which you can throw two club losers. Contract made – with an overtrick.

Please note, once again, the importance of the entries to dummy. You needed those two high spades in order to reach the dummy hand twice and attack the long suit.

Finally, you may ask, what if the diamonds had not divided equally? Then, you probably would have gone down in 4H. However, when you first looked at your two hands, you counted four losers, so it is no surprise that when your best plan fails, you still have four losers and go down. Sometimes, nothing goes right for you, but at least you tried your best.

(c) Using trumps as entries

One of the main reasons that, when you have too many losers to make your contract, you so often have to delay drawing trumps is that the trumps in dummy will serve a vital purpose; either because you can ruff losers from your hand using dummy's trumps, or because you will use the trumps as a means of access – as entries – to the dummy hand. Here's a perfect example of why you must delay drawing trumps when considering a suit establishment.

```
                   ♠ J3
                   ♥ AJ10
                   ♦ J9542
                   ♣ K53
♠ K1086                              ♠ Q9752
♥ 76                                 ♥ 43
♦ Q763                               ♦ 108
♣ QJ10                               ♣ A982
                   ♠ A4
                   ♥ KQ9852
                   ♦ AK
                   ♣ 764
```

Dealer South

N	E	S	W
–	–	1H	NB
2D	NB	3H*	NB
4H			

* the jump re-bid shows 15–18pts with a decent quality 6-card suit. North now finds it easy to raise to Game

South plays in 4H and West leads Q♣. This lead looks bad news since it means that East almost certainly holds the ace. With three club losers, you will have to find a way to avoid losing 4♠. Dummy's diamonds don't look great, but their length will prove to be their strength. However, to establish this suit, you will require multiple entries to dummy – and those can only come from AJ10 of trumps. Whatever you do with clubs, you will lose the first three tricks, after which East-

West are likely to switch to spades. You must take your A♠ or you are down. What now?

Keeping all the trumps in dummy as entries, it is time to start to establish the long suit. Cash ♦AK from hand and then cross to dummy with a low heart to 10♥. Play a low diamond and ruff it in hand. You observe that East has run out of diamonds, so West still holds Q♦. You cross back to the table with J♥ (incidentally drawing the last trumps) and lead another low diamond, again ruffing in hand. This time, West's Q♦ falls. Dummy's J♦ is now a winner and you can reach it by playing another trump to dummy's ace. On J♦ you throw 4♠ and you have made your contract.

(d) Ultimate suit establishment

Recognizing that suit quality is often unimportant if you have sufficient length will open up many new possibilities for you. If a suit contains five cards, regardless of quality, and your opponents only hold four cards, eventually that fifth card can be transformed into being a winner. This next example shows how vital that understanding can be.

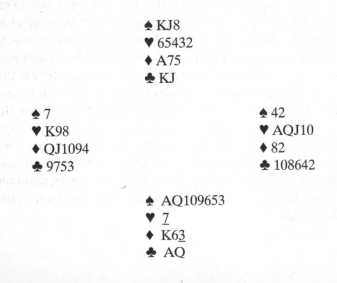

```
                  ♠ KJ8
                  ♥ 65432
                  ♦ A75
                  ♣ KJ

   ♠ 7                          ♠ 42
   ♥ K98                        ♥ AQJ10
   ♦ QJ1094                     ♦ 82
   ♣ 9753                       ♣ 108642

                  ♠ AQ109653
                  ♥ 7
                  ♦ K63
                  ♣ AQ
```

Dealer North

N	E	S	W
1H*	NB	1S	NB
2S	NB	4NT^	NB
5H#	NB	6S	

* you might prefer to open 1NT
^ Roman Key-Card Blackwood
# two key-cards, with no trump queen

South has reached 6S, against which West leads Q♦. Unfortunately, North-South's good clubs are wasted and, as well as a heart to lose, there is also a diamond. With no ruffs possible in dummy, only dummy's ghastly-looking hearts offer any hope. Can they be established? To set up a heart trick will require determination and plenty of entries to dummy. Thankfully, you have five entries: three in trumps, A♦ and K♣. You win trick one with K♦ in hand and straight away play 7♥, which East wins. East probably returns a diamond and you win with dummy's king. Now, you play a low heart from dummy and trump it with a high trump in your own hand. You must trump high, both to ensure that you are not over-trumped, but also to preserve low trumps in your hand to overtake in dummy as entries. Next, play a low trump to dummy and lead another heart. Again, ruff this in hand with a high trump. A♥ is still outstanding, so you must repeat this process once more. Go to dummy's K♠ (all the trumps have been safely drawn by now) and lead a fourth heart from the table; East produces A♥, and you ruff once more. Now, there in dummy, sits 6♥. Since no one holds any more hearts, it is a winner. You cross to dummy with Q♣ to K♣ and lead your brilliantly established 6♥ to throw away your losing diamond from hand. You claim your slam, having performed some pure bridge magic.

Ruffs and Over-Ruffs

Notice that, in each of the examples above, whether ruffing in dummy, using dummy's winning cards, or establishing dummy's long suit, you are unlikely to be able to draw trumps before undertaking your play to create extra tricks, or discard losers.

There are a few hands where you can safely draw trumps and then make your planned play for extra tricks but, almost always, you must leave your opponents with trumps in their hands while you make your play. Whilst this appears dangerous, it is a perfectly reasonable risk to take: after all, you have assessed your losers and, if you draw trumps, those are the cards you will lose. So, by delaying drawing trumps, and seeking ruffs or a suit establishment, you are trying to make a contract which, otherwise, would fail. If your opponents unexpectedly ruff in and you go down by two tricks rather than just one, so be it. At least you failed trying to succeed.

If you can afford to trump high while ruffing in dummy or trying for a suit establishment, then this will add to the safety of your play. If your trumps are not sufficiently strong to trump high each time, then, if you plan to trump more than once, trump low the first time (when it is less likely that an opponent can over-ruff) and ruff with a higher trumps on subsequent occasions (when it is more likely that your opponents are exhausted in the suit and might over-ruff).

(e)

<pre>
                        ♠ Q94
                        ♥ A86
                        ♦ J5
                        ♣ A6432
    ♠ A5   ♠ 632
    ♥ QJ104   ♥ K73
    ♦ Q10987   ♦ 62
    ♣ 97   ♣ KJ1085
                        ♠ KJ108<u>7</u>
                        ♥ 95<u>2</u>
                        ♦ AK<u>43</u>
                        ♣ Q
</pre>

Dealer South

N	E	S	W
–	–	1S	NB
2C	NB	2D	NB
3S*	NB	4S	

*the jump to 3S shows 10–12pts with 3-card spades support. Had North bid only 2S this would have indicated too weak a hand.

You reach an ambitious contract of 4S and West leads Q♥. With five losers, you realize that you will have to trump two diamonds in dummy (you don't have enough clubs between you to form two discards via suit establishment). You must delay drawing trumps since you will need two in dummy for your ruffs. At trick two, you play 5♦ from dummy and win with A♦. You cash K♦ and lead 3♦. Notice that, if you trump this card with dummy's 4♠, East will over-ruff with his 6♠ and lead another trump. West will win his A♠ and lead 5♠, removing all trumps from dummy and leaving you two down. Since you have all the high trumps apart from the Ace, you can afford to trump this first diamond with 9♠ and, having returned to hand by playing A♣ and ruffing a low club, then trump 4♦ with Q♠. This way, East could only over-ruff with A♠ (if he had held it) and that is a loser for you anyway.

So, here, you can afford to trump high each time and, to succeed, you must do so.

Apart from ruffs and suit establishments, there are, of course, other methods of creating extra tricks or avoiding losers, but these rarely occur and are really the preserve of experts. If you can ruff safely in dummy and establish a long suit with regard to preserving entries, you'll be an awesome declarer in suit contracts.

You can also rely on your opponents giving you tricks from time to time. Sometimes, when defending, it is difficult to avoid giving away tricks but, more often, players just defend poorly.

Finally, as your levels of experience and ability rise, you will find yourself being able to foresee problems and fend them off, observe your opponents' cards and judge their actions accurately, and most of all, form coherent, reasonable plans of attack whenever you are the declarer.

For now, however, let's switch roles to that of defenders, and see how to slow down the progress of declarers and thwart their plans.

Suit Contracts – The Defence
Remember, there are only three ways the declarer can try to avoid the consequences of holding losers:

1. Trumping them in dummy.

2. Discarding them on dummy's long suit.

3. Finessing, or hoping for the defence's help.

How can you stop him achieving the first of these techniques? When the dummy contains a shortage, the declarer's likely objective is to trump that suit with dummy's trumps. Therefore, with the aim of wanting to use up dummy's, you should lead trumps at the earliest possible opportunity.

Let's take a look at a full example from which you should be able to see clearly the effect of this counter-attack.

South plays in 2S, and West leads Q♥:

```
                    ♠ 10965
                    ♥ K632
                    ♦ Q87
                    ♣ J9
 ♠ 2                                      ♠ A43
 ♥ QJ10                                   ♥ A954
 ♦ J432                                   ♦ K1065
 ♣ Q10875                                 ♣ K3
                    ♠ KQJ87
                    ♥ 87
                    ♦ A9
                    ♣ A642
```

Declarer's losers are underlined, and come to a total of seven – two more than he can afford. His plan will be to ruff two of his club losers with dummy's trumps, before drawing the opponents' trumps. If the defence sit back, that is what he will do, and he will emerge triumphant with his eight tricks. Instead, both defenders should spot the doubleton club in dummy, and suspect that declarer will want to make use of the shortage by ruffing clubs in dummy. If Q♥ is allowed to hold the trick, as it should be – in an attempt to score K♥ later – then West should switch to a trump at trick 2. East wins with A♠, and returns another trump. Declarer wins, but is only left with two trumps in dummy. He still tries to carry out his plan, by playing A♣, and another, leaving a void in dummy. East wins this second club trick, and plays off his final trump. Now, dummy is left with only one trump, and declarer is able to trump only one of his two other losing clubs. As all his other losers are unavoidable, he will now go one down in a contract he would frequently have been allowed to make. So:

> *When declarer wants to trump losers in dummy,*
> *defenders must lead trumps as often as possible.*

Now, what should the defenders' strategy be when there is a long suit in dummy? Once again, you must put yourself into the mind of the declarer to thwart his plans. At the table you are not in a position to be able to see all the hands so, before looking at the full example, see whether you can anticipate the look of the opponents' hands by listening to the bidding.

The declarer is South. You are West:

N	E	S	W	
–	–	1S	NB	It sounds as if South must hold at
2D	NB	2S	NB	least six good spades, and North six good diamonds. That means that
3D	NB	4S	NB	South will be able to discard all his
NB	NB			losers on those long diamonds unless your side take your tricks quickly.

Therefore, you should make an attacking lead in one of the un-bid suits, hoping to make four tricks before declarer gains the lead.

Let's see if the hands turn out as expected:

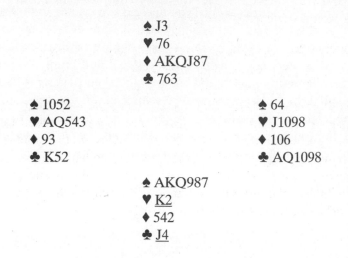

♠ J3
♥ 76
♦ AKQJ87
♣ 763

♠ 1052   ♠ 64
♥ AQ543   ♥ J1098
♦ 93   ♦ 106
♣ K52   ♣ AQ1098

♠ AKQ987
♥ K2
♦ 542
♣ J4

Yes, it is all pretty much as anticipated. Watch what happens if you, sitting West, make a passive lead of a trump. Declarer wins, draws the outstanding trumps, and then plays off all his diamonds, emerging with a total of twelve tricks. Three of his four losers are just thrown away on the diamonds.

If, instead, you lead one of the un-bid suits, you may be able to make four tricks before declarer gets a look in. It would be unwise to lead a heart from a holding headed by AQ, so you lead a small club. East wins, sees the threatening solid diamond suit in dummy, and switches to a heart. He chooses J♥, as top of a sequence is right (see page 192), hoping to find you with something. Whatever card South plays, you can win, then cash a second heart trick, and also win with K♣. This way, your side has made the first four tricks, and declarer ends up one down.

When dummy contains a long suit,
attack the un-bid suits very aggressively.

Sometimes it will be necessary to find the right opening lead whilst, on other occasions, you may get the chance to find the right defence later on, having seen dummy. Next time your opponents are bidding, don't just sit there bemoaning your poor fortune, try to work out the shape and point count of their hands and, later, how many points your partner is likely to hold. In this way, you will give yourself a far better chance of defeating the contract.

So, you have seen the two occasions when you have to take positive action in defence against a suit contract:

Leading trumps when there is a shortage in dummy

and

Attacking un-bid suits when there is a long suit in dummy.

However, the above types of hand only account for about a third of all the defences you make. The majority of hands fall into the third category we identified at the outset (see page 176). With no shortages or long suit in dummy, declarer has no chance of getting rid of losers, other than by finessing or hoping for a defensive error. On these occasions it is vital that you adopt a safe, passive defence.

N	E	S	W	
				South is the declarer. You are West.
NB	NB	1S	NB	From the auction it sounds as if North
1NT	NB	4S	NB	holds a weak balanced hand, and
NB	NB			South has bid optimistically to Game.

Certainly, it does not sound as if there are shortages or long suits in dummy. So, your aim should be a passive, careful defence, not giving anything away.

Try to work out what you should lead against this contract, holding the following hand:

♠ Q52   At first sight, you might be tempted to lead J♥
♥ J3   from your doubleton. This aggressive lead could
♦ QJ109   give the contract to South who could mark East
♣ AQ98   with Q♥, and later finesse against him for an extra
           trick. Have you worked out how many points your
partner is likely to hold? He cannot possibly hold ♥AK – you
have 12pts, and your opponents are in Game (for which they
are likely to hold about 26 HCP). A trump is a possible lead
for you, but most unwise from Qxx. The best lead is Q♦ – top
of a sequence. It is an attacking lead, because it will eventually push out ♦AK to establish a trick, but completely safe, as
it cannot give anything away. In fact, it is the only lead to give
you a chance.

Here is the full deal:

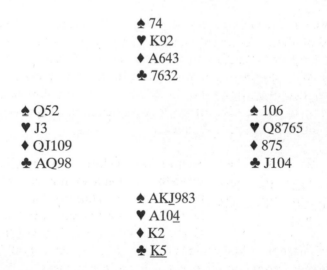

```
                    ♠ 74
                    ♥ K92
                    ♦ A643
                    ♣ 7632

  ♠ Q52                          ♠ 106
  ♥ J3                           ♥ Q8765
  ♦ QJ109                        ♦ 875
  ♣ AQ98                         ♣ J104

                    ♠ AKJ983
                    ♥ A104
                    ♦ K2
                    ♣ K5
```

Provided that between you and your partner, you don't help
declarer, he will have to lose a spade, a heart, and two clubs.
Your side just keeps leading diamonds whenever you get in,
letting declarer trump in his own hand.

It is almost always right to make declarer trump in his own hand – it doesn't give him any extra tricks, it just shortens his trump holding.

On the hand above, if you lead any of the other suits at any time, you will give the declarer the extra trick that he needs.

With a balanced dummy, keep leading the safest cards you can find (i.e. top of a sequence, or a suit that makes declarer trump in his own hand). If there is no long suit in dummy on which declarer can throw away losers, <u>there cannot be any hurry</u>.

This is the type of defence which seems to cause the most problems, with defenders scurrying from suit to suit, trying to make tricks quickly. I repeat (because it is so vital):

If there is no long suit in dummy, there is no hurry to cash tricks.

Leads Against Suit Contracts

I could fill ten books on this subject, but you will find that experience is the best guide. Above all, listen to the bidding.

Here are six key guidelines to keep at the forefront of your mind:

1. **Lead top of a sequence** if you have one. This lead combines attack with safety, and also informs partner. If you lead a King, you promise the Queen; if you lead a Jack, you promise the 10; and the 10 promises the 9. With lower cards than that, however, it doesn't count – leading an 8 does not promise the 7.

2. **Don't lead a doubleton**. Unless your partner has bid the suit, or obviously holds a lot of points, it is a very risky play that costs, much more often than it gains. This is because

you are forcing your partner to play from his hand, before declarer has to play. Consequently, any high cards held by your partner can be beaten by declarer whom, you should assume, is most likely to be strong.

3. **Lead your partner's suit**. If your partner has bid, then you should lead his suit unless you have a much better idea – a singleton perhaps. When you do lead partner's suit, lead top of a sequence if you have one, otherwise follow the rules below. Don't lead the highest card in partner's suit for the sake of it.

4. **Lead a low card to show interest in the suit; lead a higher card to show lack of interest in the suit**. The lead of a low card suggests that you hold an honour at the head of the suit, whilst a higher card would deny an honour. For example, from ♦K852, you should lead the 2♦, but from ♦9732, you should lead 7♦. In this way, partner will have some idea of your holding.

5. **Never lead away from an Ace**; i.e. do not lead a little card from a holding headed by the Ace. As you must not lead an Ace without holding the King, this means that if you hold ♦A852, you should not lead the suit at all. Just wait for partner or declarer to lead it.

6. **Lead trumps if other leads seem unappealing**, but don't lead a singleton trump as you may spoil your partner's holding. If you are short in trumps, partner probably has three or four. If you leave declarer in the dark about the fact that the trumps are splitting badly, you will have more chance of your partner scoring tricks with his length in trumps.

In suit contracts then, deciding whether to attack, or remain passive and let declarer find his own way, is often a delicate matter. In NT contracts battle is much more open and aggressive. This is because the success of both declarer and the defence rests on the same simple strategy: who can get his long suit(s) established and producing tricks first. It is a straight race for the tricks.

The good news is that declarer and defence are in face-to-face confrontation and the aggressive nearly always win. So you know upon which side to err.

NT Contracts – The Declarer

Declarer's technique in NT contracts is only slightly different from that in a suit contract. The key difference is that, in your assessment of the hand in a NT contract, you should be counting <u>tricks</u> rather than losers. Also, in contrast to counting losers for a suit contract, here you <u>do</u> count all tricks that dummy can contribute. The other questions: your combined point count, and what that leaves for the defence; what your opponents have bid; analysis of the opening lead; are all just as relevant as before.

Let's look at an example to illustrate the basic principles:

♠ Q53
♥ 87
♦ KQJ98
♣ A52

6♣ led

♠ A52
♥ A432
♦ 1065
♣ KQ3

Sitting South, you deal and open 1NT, and your partner raises you to 3NT hoping that his 5-card diamond suit will pull its weight. After the lead, you want to count <u>top tricks</u>, that is to say, tricks that you can make *off the top* or straightaway.

On this hand, you have the following top tricks:

A♠   = 1 trick
A♥   = 1 trick
♣AKQ   = 3 tricks

and nothing in diamonds yet.

So far then, you have got five certain tricks and, as you are in 3NT, this means that you require a further four tricks from somewhere.

Once you have assessed how many top tricks you have, decide from which suit or suits you will find the extra tricks you require for your contract. Attack those immediately.

Your extra tricks will nearly always come from the suit in which you hold the most cards between both hands. In this instance, diamonds will obviously provide those four tricks, once you have dislodged A♦. Your plan then is to push out A♦ before doing anything else. Most importantly, you must not play out the high cards in the other suits before pushing out A♦, otherwise your opponents will be able to cash lots of tricks in those suits when they gain the lead with A♦. Hence, we have a rule:

In NTs, never cash any top tricks until you have enough tricks to make your contract.

Of course, you will have to part with winners in order to gain the lead when your opponents play a suit. However, the point of this rule is to dissuade you from releasing <u>stoppers</u> – the high cards at the top of the suit – which prevent your opponents from cashing tricks with their small cards until you have enough tricks for your contract.

Now, if we look at the full layout of these cards, you can see how your campaign should work.

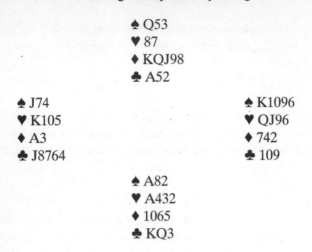

Win the 6♣ lead, in your own hand, preserving A♣ in dummy, as it has comparatively few high cards, and immediately start leading diamonds, continuing until West takes his A♦. Win whatever he returns and, now that you have your nine tricks, cash them and claim your contract.

If you had played off your A♥ and A♠ before losing A♦, E/W could have cashed three heart tricks and three spade tricks before you regained the lead. (West can lead a spade through dummy's remaining holding of ♠Qx, and East will pounce on Q♠ with his K♠, or win the trick cheaply with his 9♠.)

When playing off a long suit there is a danger you will end up in the wrong hand, which is known as "blocking" yourself. To avoid this, simply remember:

When playing off a long suit,
play the high card from the shorter holding each time.

In the example below, if you play ♥AQ from dummy first, you will then be forced to win the third round with your K♥, leaving you with no further hearts to cash in your hand.

Obeying the rule above ensures that you will end up in the hand with long suit, able to cash all the available tricks.

Your hand   ♥ K63   ♥ AQJ98   Dummy

Sometimes you may end up in the wrong hand because there are not enough entries (high cards to gain you access to one hand or the other) to allow you to cash your tricks. This hand is typical:

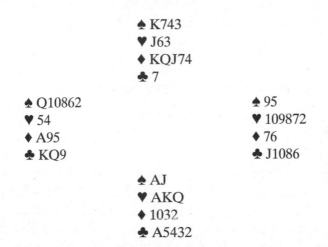

```
                    ♠ K743
                    ♥ J63
                    ♦ KQJ74
                    ♣ 7
  ♠ Q10862                      ♠ 95
  ♥ 54                          ♥ 109872
  ♦ A95                         ♦ 76
  ♣ KQ9                         ♣ J1086
                    ♠ AJ
                    ♥ AKQ
                    ♦ 1032
                    ♣ A5432
```

You, as South, open 1C, and end up declarer in 3NT. West leads 6♠. Once again, you should count your top tricks. You have:

Three, in spades (now that small spade has been led to you)
Three, in hearts
None, in diamonds
One, in clubs.

So, you can see seven certain top tricks and, as before, the long diamond suit should provide the extra you require. However, when you play a small spade from dummy, and East plays only 9♠, you should hesitate before winning with J♠. If you win with J♠, you will have only the bare A♠ in your hand, and you may no longer be able to gain access to dummy. If, when you play the diamonds, West refuses to play A♦ until the third round, you will have no diamonds left in your own hand, and no way of getting to dummy to cash the remaining two winners, leaving you a trick short.

The solution is to win trick 1 with A♠, immediately play diamonds until A♦ is played, regain the lead, and cross to dummy with K♠ to cash your tricks. This way nothing can stop you from making ten tricks, one more than you need, instead of one short. Therefore:

> *When setting up a long suit, always ensure that you retain*
> *sufficient means of entry into that hand.*

A little thought at the start is all it required to solve the problem.

As with suit contracts, remembering if/what your opponents have bid can be important to the success of the contract. Analysis of the lead plays a vital role as well (see leads against NTs, page 212) as you can see from this example:

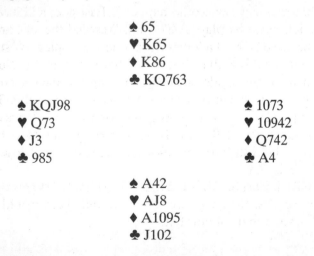

```
                    ♠ 65
                    ♥ K65
                    ♦ K86
                    ♣ KQ763
    ♠ KQJ98                         ♠ 1073
    ♥ Q73                           ♥ 10942
    ♦ J3                            ♦ Q742
    ♣ 985                           ♣ A4
                    ♠ A42
                    ♥ AJ8
                    ♦ A1095
                    ♣ J102
```

You, South, open 1NT, partner bids 2NT, and you raise to 3NT. West leads K♠. Now, you count your top tricks:

One, in spades
Two, in hearts
Two, in diamonds
None, in clubs.

So, you have five top tricks, and a further four will come from clubs once A♣ is dislodged. Entries to dummy are in good supply, so the only thing to worry about is that your opponents have all the top spades except for A♠. If you were to win the first trick with A♠, you would then play clubs immediately, but when East won with A♣, he would return a spade, and you would go down, losing A♣ and four spade tricks.

If, instead, you were to refuse to take your A♠ until the third round then, when East then won with A♣, he would have no spades left to return to his partner; you could win any other suit, and cash out to a total of nine tricks. That, as you can see, is the winning technique. It is called "holding up". The effect is to exhaust one opponent of his supply of the danger suit.

What, you may say, would happen if East does still have a spade left when he plays A♣? Well, West led the suit originally because he held a long suit that he was hoping to establish, so it is unlikely that East would have four spades. But if he had, then their spades would be splitting 4-4, and you could only lose three spade tricks and A♣, whatever you did. The "hold-up" play of not releasing A♠ for two rounds was to guard against the likely bad distribution of the suit. Note that whatever the distribution of the spades, you cannot lose by making this play.

Finally, it must be admitted that if West holds A♣ as well as all the spades, then you are defeated, but there would be nothing you can do about that.

When you hold only one stopper in a suit, it is usually wise to "hold-up" that card for as long as possible in order to exhaust at least one opponent of his supply of the suit.

As you become more experienced, you will be able to judge for how long to hold-up a single stopper, since there are times when to hold-up for only one round (or two rounds) may be the correct play.

There are many other techniques required for success in no-trump contracts, but there is one which can transform your understanding of the play of the cards. Although it is predominantly a technique for NT success, similar plays also occur in suit contracts. If you can master this technique, you will be in a very strong position to bring home many more of your contracts.

Avoidance

The principle of "Avoidance" is this: one opponent often presents more of a threat to you than his partner. If you can identify that dangerous opponent and prevent him from gaining the lead, you will be able to nullify the threat. Let's see a simple example first:

(a)

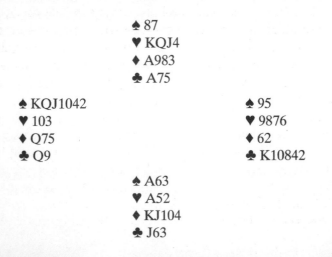

Dealer East

N	E	S	W
–	NB	1NT	NB
2C*	NB	2D^	NB
3NT			

*Stayman, seeking a 4-4 heart fit
^ no 4-card major suit

Against South's 3NT contract, West leads top-of-a-sequence K♠. You count your tricks: one spade, four hearts, two diamonds and one club – eight tricks. Your diamond suit will provide one further trick. Your only problem is that you hold only one spade stopper. Let's see what we can do...

You hold-up your A♠ until the third round, noting that East shows out after two rounds of the suit. Now you know that West holds three more spade winners and, if he were to gain the lead before you had fulfilled your contract, you will be defeated. He is very definitely the "danger hand" and must be kept off lead.

As usual in NT contracts, you must tackle your extra tricks before enjoying the easy ones, so you must attack the diamond suit immediately. Since you do not mind if East, the "safe hand", takes a trick, you can relax about him. However, you cannot allow West to win a trick, so you must focus on that objective. As you are only missing Q♦, you can finesse against this card, assuming that West holds it (if East has it, you don't mind if he wins with it – he has no spades left to lead).

Lead J♦ from your hand and, if West covers with Q♦, you can win in dummy with A♦. If West plays low on your J♦, you can play low from dummy too. Now that West cannot win the trick, you are safe to take that risk. On this deal, East cannot beat your J♦, so the finesse succeeds and you will make your 3NT contract with ease. Even if East could take Q♦, he has no spades left to lead and whatever else he plays, you can win, and your 10♦ is your ninth trick. Your contract is 100 per cent safe.

Because this is such a vital technique, if you don't feel happy about this example, I urge you to lay out all four hands, using a pack of cards, and play through the deal again, following the suggested play. Once you are happy with this principle, you can move on to some more complicated avoidance plays.

In that first example, it was completely obvious which opponent presented the danger: West held all the remaining spades and had the power to defeat you should he gain the lead. In the next examples, in order to identify the dangerous opponent, you must analyse the play to the first trick and envision what might happen later on in the hand.

(b)

                    ♠ Q6
                    ♥ A85
                    ♦ AKJ63
                    ♣ 1095

    ♠ AJ932   ♠ 1074
    ♥ 962   ♥ J1043
    ♦ 72   ♦ Q84
    ♣ K84   ♣ 732

                    ♠ K85
                    ♥ KQ7
                    ♦ 1095
                    ♣ AQJ6

Dealer South

N	E	S	W
–	–	1C	NB
1D	NB	1NT*	NB
3NT			

*15/16pts, balanced hand

West leads his fourth highest card from his longest suit – 3♠ – and you count your tricks. You have one spade coming in a moment, three hearts, two diamonds and a club. That is seven tricks, so you need to develop two more. It is nearly always right to play the doubleton honour from dummy when you have the queen and king between your two hands, so you rise with Q♠ at trick one and it holds the trick. Now is the time to visualize your opponents' hands. These are the questions you must ask yourself: Who holds A♠? Which opponent threatens your remaining ♠K8 more? How can you keep that opponent from gaining the lead?

Let's look at each in turn:

Who holds A♠?
West certainly holds it – for one simple reason: if East had held it, he would definitely have played it. When your partner leads a low card, he is asking you to try to win the trick and return the suit to you. If East could have done, he would have done.

Which opponent threatens your remaining ♠K8 more?
At first glance, you might think that it is West; after all, he holds the spade length. But, if you ask yourself which spade West could lead that would hurt you, you'll find that your K♠ is quite safe. If West leads A♠, your K♠ wins later; if he leads a low spade, your K♠ wins immediately. In fact, it is East who poses the danger: he can lead a spade through your ♠K8, making you decide whether to play your King or your 8 before West has to choose which card he has to play. If East leads a spade through your hand, you will lose the next four tricks and go down.

How can you keep him off lead?
Simply – don't let him win a trick. That will involve ensuring that he cannot win a finesse taken into his hand. Instead, you

should finesse <u>through</u> his hand, ensuring that whatever card he plays, you can beat it.

Now, let's put all this thinking together into a simple plan. Normally, you would attack the suit in which you hold most cards between your two hands. In this case, that would mean diamonds. However, missing Q♦, you would have to finesse through the West hand and risk losing to East. This, we have decided, is an unacceptable risk. Instead, look at the club suit. Whether the finesse wins or loses, you will certainly develop two extra tricks – without risking East gaining the lead.

So, having taken trick one with Q♠, lead 10♣ from dummy. If East were to play the Queen, you would win and your extra tricks would be made. As it is, East plays low, and so do you. West wins with K♣, but cannot lead another spade without giving you a trick, nor lead any other suit without you being able to win and fulfil your contract. Once again, with some careful thought, you have made your contract a certainty.

As a general rule, remember that:

When finessing, make sure that you play <u>through</u> the danger hand, only risking losing to the safe hand.

In other words:

Make the danger hand play first (out of your two opponents) to any trick where you might lose, ensuring that you cover any card played by the danger hand.

Let's see another example:

(c)

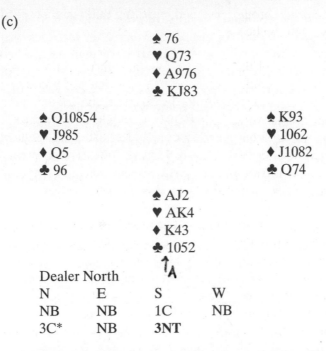

♠ 76
♥ Q73
♦ A976
♣ KJ83

♠ Q10854
♥ J985
♦ Q5
♣ 96

♠ K93
♥ 1062
♦ J1082
♣ Q74

♠ AJ2
♥ AK4
♦ K43
♣ 1052

Dealer North

N	E	S	W
NB	NB	1C	NB
3C*	NB	**3NT**	

*a 1D response is a reasonable alternative but, since that is only a minor suit, supporting partner immediately is probably superior.

Against South's 3NT, West leads 5♠. Declarer counts his tricks: one spade, three hearts, two diamonds and two clubs: eight tricks. One more is required and it can certainly be made in the club suit (you have both J♣ and 10♣). East plays K♠ to trick one and you decide to win. Your ♠J2 is now open to attack if East is allowed to lead a spade through your hand back to West. However, it is protected if West is on lead, so East is the danger hand. When you come to tackle clubs, you must do so in such a way that East cannot gain the lead. Following the rules above therefore, you should play a low club from hand to dummy's K♣ and then a low club from dummy, covering whatever card East plays. That way, he cannot win the trick. As it happens, this finesse succeeds and you should make 3NT with an overtrick.

Incidentally, you could have played this hand differently. If you had held up your A♠ instead of winning the first trick, you can form a different position. Imagine that you duck the first two rounds of spades, winning the third. Now, East is exhausted of spades and can be considered a safe hand, whereas West holds two further spade winners and is now the danger hand.

In this scenario, you must take the club finesse the other way around: lead a low club from your hand, covering whatever card West plays. Here, East would win with Q♣, but he has no spades left to lead and therefore cannot harm you. Your contract makes again.

Generally, if you hold up your stopper until the last round, it will be the opponent who led the suit who will be the danger hand whereas, if you win the first trick, it will be the partner of the leader who will be the danger hand, as he will have the power to lead back that suit to his partner through your remaining holding.

This next example shows, once again, how important it is to make a plan of attack before deciding what to do at trick one: it may affect your thinking completely:

(d)

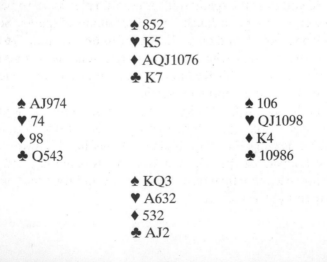

      ♠ 852
      ♥ K5
      ♦ AQJ1076
      ♣ K7

♠ AJ974   ♠ 106
♥ 74   ♥ QJ1098
♦ 98   ♦ K4
♣ Q543   ♣ 10986

      ♠ KQ3
      ♥ A632
      ♦ 532
      ♣ AJ2

Dealer North

N	E	S	W
1D	NB	1H*	NB
2D	NB	**3NT**	

*it is essential to show any 4-card major in response at the 1-level if you can.

West leads 7♠ against your contract. It is obvious that you will want to establish dummy's lovely, long diamond suit, but you may have problems in spades. Sure enough, when you play low from dummy, East contributes 10♠ (confirming that he does not hold A♠). You are now faced with a tough decision: if you win this trick with Q♠, you will be left ♠K3 and, if East gains the lead later, he will return a spade through your hand to West's waiting Ace. The problem for you is that when you tackle diamonds, you have no choice but to finesse into the East hand. That seems way too much of a risk. Is there an alternative?

Since you have to take the finesse into the East hand – and if the finesse succeeds then even my cat can make 3NT – you must assume that it is wrong and that East will win. How else could you treat the spade suit? A hold-up play looks to be the answer, in order to exhaust East of his supply of spades. So, at trick one, you should duck! East returns 6♠, you play Q♠ and now whether West wins his A♠ or not, East has no spades left. When you lose to his K♦ later, you control whatever he leads instead and your contract is secure.

By the way, if East holds three spades, then your hold-up may not work, since West can duck the second round of spades, leaving East with a spade in his hand. However, if East holds three spades, then West holds only four, and you cannot lose more than three spade tricks and K♦. Once again, your contract is secure.

Sometimes, as in the above example, there is only one way you can possibly take a finesse and, if that finesse risks losing to the dangerous opponent, you must seek possible alternatives. Cover up the East-West hands on this next deal, and ask yourself how you might play in 3NT, when West leads 6♥.

(e)

```
                    ♠ AQ
                    ♥ 852
                    ♦ 1074
                    ♣ AK753
  ♠ 109                           ♠ J87653
  ♥ KJ964                         ♥ Q10
  ♦ Q3                            ♦ 952
  ♣ J1082                         ♣ Q9
                    ♠ K42
                    ♥ A73
                    ♦ AKJ86
                    ♣ 64
```

Dealer South

N	E	S	W
–	–	1D	NB
2C	NB	2NT*	NB
3NT			

*much superior to re-bidding 2D, which would show a much weaker hand than your 15/16pts.

West's 6♥ lead has hit your weakest spot. However, you have three spade tricks, a heart, two diamonds and two club tricks – that is eight tricks. So, you have only to find one more trick. The diamond suit looks the most promising. Let's see what happens in the early tricks: with only one stopper in hearts, you duck the first trick, and the second, and win the third round – noting that East has now shown out. So, West holds two more heart winners, whilst East can be safely allowed on lead, since he is exhausted of hearts. How best to play the diamonds?

The one thing you must definitely **not** do is to finesse into the West hand. That should be avoided at all costs (on a few hands, there is simply no other alternative but to risk it). Instead, at trick four, lay down A♦ and K♦. As it is, West's Q♦ falls and now you make the rest of the tricks but, had it not, you could still play a third round, hoping that East held the Queen. If he did, you would still succeed. If West holds ♦Qxx, then you cannot succeed – it's just unlucky. The key is not to lose to a singleton or doubleton Queen – that would be careless.

By the way, if you do play a third round of diamonds and East wins with his Queen, your opponent or partner will probably point out – usually pompously – that you could have finessed and not lost to the Queen in the East hand. My advice is not to bother to explain why you played the hand correctly – it will probably be lost on him.

The final example is one of my favourite hands of all time, simply because until I first saw it, it never occurred to me that such a play could exist. It's another little piece of bridge magic and the technique required occurs surprisingly often, both in no-trump and suit contracts. It never had a proper name, so I christened it a "Stranding Play" in an early book and now that seems to have become the accepted term for it.

(f)

```
                      ♠ 74
                      ♥ AK54
                      ♦ 8743
                      ♣ AQ6
   ♠ KJ963                          ♠ Q85
   ♥ J983                           ♥ Q10
   ♦ J106                           ♦ Q5
   ♣ 7                             ♣ 985432
                      ♠ A102
                      ♥ 762
                      ♦ AK92
                      ♣ KJ10
```

Dealer South

N	E	S	W
–	–	1D	NB
1H	NB	1NT	NB
3NT*			

*You are taking a risk in spades by supporting no-trumps directly – and there are alternatives – but life is full of risks and this is a perfectly reasonable one to take.

West leads 6♠ against your contract and, counting your tricks (one spade, two hearts, two diamonds and three clubs) you realize that you have eight, and require one more. The diamond suit seems the most likely source but, if you simply cash ♦AK, West will win the third round with his J♦ and cash his remaining spade winners. How can that problem be solved?

You duck the first two rounds of spades, winning the third, leaving East without any further spades. He is now a safe hand to allow on lead, whereas West is dangerous since he holds two more spade winners. To establish the diamonds,

you will not be able to avoid West from gaining the lead –
since you can't play through his hand – but you might be able
to strand East on lead instead. Let's see the play in action.

At trick four, you cross to dummy with a heart to A♥. You
lead a low diamond and, when East plays small, you have to
win to avoid West gaining the lead. You return to dummy,
perhaps this time with A♣ and lead a second low diamond.
This time, East must play Q♦ and on that you... duck, leaving
East on lead with his Q♦ and unable to lead any more spades.
Later, when you play K♦, West's J♦ will fall and your fourth
low diamond will be a winner and your ninth trick.

If Q♦ does not appear on the second round, you will have
to win again in hand and play out a third diamond, hoping
that it is East who holds the final card. If West started with
♦Qxx, you cannot make the contract.

By the way, playing A♦ and then a low diamond should not
work. If I was sitting in the East seat and you led A♦, I would
throw Q♦ under it. I'd do this because I'd know that my
partner was desperate to re-gain the lead to cash his spade
winners and I'd be doing everything I could to get rid of my
high cards in order to promote his lower cards into winners.

Over many years of teaching, I have found that understanding avoidance techniques is one of the hardest elements of
card play for students. I think that if you lay out the cards on
a table in front of you and play out the deals above, you should
have the best possible chance of understanding the key principles. Once you have mastered them, you will look back on
any confusion you may have suffered with astonishment – it's
not really that difficult.

Incidentally, avoidance plays – like so many more advanced
bridge techniques – require you to ask several questions about
the hand, your opponents' play, and your own strategy. At
first, this may seem daunting but, in fact, each of those questions is really quite simple to answer. The problem is that you
have to deal with several of them at once, all the while keeping
focused on what is happening at the table. Practice will

undoubtedly boost your confidence and soon you will start to spot the influence of these plays in very many hands with which you are confronted every time you sit down to play.

NT Contracts – The Defence

When defending suit contracts, you often need to have seen dummy before you can work out much of the plan declarer may be attempting, and only then can you begin to counter his play.

Against NT contracts, your strategy is simpler, because you know what the declarer will be trying to do – set up a long suit to provide extra tricks – and you will be trying to do exactly the same. You have a slight advantage over the declarer as you are able to lead your long suit first.

If your partner has bid a suit during the auction, you should automatically lead it. Failing that, it is right to lead your own longest suit against a NT contract, provided that it has not been bid by your opposition.

Having decided upon the correct suit, there are three main types of lead you can make:

I   Top of a Sequence.
II   The fourth highest card in the suit.
III High card from a poor holding.

I TOP OF A SEQUENCE

A "Sequence" of cards in NTs means three high cards in a row.

There are four different types of sequence lead available.

(a) Top of a Sequence

<u>K</u>QJ74, <u>Q</u>J1043, <u>A</u>KQ2, <u>10</u>9842, 6543

It would be correct to lead the top card from all of the above combinations, except for the last one. Sequences headed by 10 are the lowest which count. After that the sequence is not important enough to bother with.

(b) Top of a Broken Sequence

A Broken Sequence is two high cards in sequence, plus the next but one in sequence.

K̲Q10532,   J̲10842,   A̲KJ4,   Q̲J932

All the above holdings are headed by a broken sequence, and it is correct to lead the top card in each instance.

Therefore, when partner sees Q led against a NT contract, he knows that you also hold J10, or J9. This information, which is also available to declarer, often proves vital in defeating the contract.

(c) Top of an Internal Sequence

An Internal Sequence is just a sequence that appears inside a suit holding, with one high card above it.

AJ̲1098,   KJ̲10952,   Q1̲0̲983,   AQJ̲105

The correct lead in each case is, once again, underlined.

(d) Top of an Internal Broken Sequence

This is just the internal version of the broken sequence lead.

AJ̲1084,   Q1̲0̲9762,   KJ̲1083,   AQJ̲9

When partner leads J, he therefore promises 109 or 108, *and* his suit *may* also contain one card higher than J. This card cannot be Q however, because then he would have led Q from QJ10.

II FOURTH HIGHEST CARD IN THE SUIT

This lead is the traditional one to be made at all times when the suit you have chosen contains no sequence. If you have a sequence of high cards, then you must lead top of this sequence rather than fourth highest. Top of a sequence is a safer lead because declarer must win with a card higher than the top of your sequence, whereas after a fourth highest lead, if your partner holds no high cards in the suit, declarer will win the trick cheaply with a low card.

As you become even more experienced, both as declarer and a defender, there are many complicated inferences to be taken from a fourth highest lead.

(a) KJ7<u>4</u>2,   (b) AQ9<u>6</u>3,   (c) Q108<u>4</u>,   (d) QJ7<u>5</u>3,   (e) J64<u>3</u>2

In each holding above, a fourth highest lead is correct.

Notice in (b) that it is acceptable to lead away from an Ace. You would not do this against a suit contract but, against a NT contract, the risk of giving away a cheap trick is outweighed by the need to get to work on your long suit as quickly as possible.

In (d), the suit is headed by QJ but there is no 9 or 10, so these two cards alone do not constitute a sequence. Against a suit contract, it would be acceptable to lead Q from this holding, because you are trying to win tricks quickly before the declarer starts trumping.

The golden rule is:

In suit contracts <u>two</u> high cards in a row constitute a sequence from which you should lead the high card.
In NT contracts, you require <u>three</u> significant cards for the holding to be regarded as a sequence.

The main exception to leading your own longest suit is when you hold a very weak hand. Imagine that your opposition's bidding has run 1NT – 2NT – 3NT, and you are on lead holding this hand:

♠ J5   To lead your own long suit here would be point-
♥ 8532   less. Even if partner can help you to establish it,
♦ 97532   you have no entries with which to regain the lead.
♣ 85   A much better idea would be to try to lead *part-
            ner's* longest suit. The opposition have 25 or
26pts, you hold 1pt, so partner has at least 13pts with which
later to gain the lead. You can only guess in which suit he
might have length but, as your opposition have not used
Stayman, it may well be that they do not have a good fit in a
major suit. I would therefore recommend leading J♠. By
looking at dummy and his own hand, plus the bidding, partner
should be able to work out firstly, that you are very weak, and
secondly, that you cannot hold a long spade suit. If partner
holds five spades – as he well might – you will be the hero of
the day. On the occasions when your brilliance misses the
target, be philosophical – your time will come... One thing is
certain:

*When you are very weak, you must not lead your own long suit.
Lead your strongest short suit, hoping to find partner with
length, and the entries to establish it.*

III HIGH CARD FROM A POOR HOLDING

This last lead is important as it differentiates between a suit
headed by an honour, when you would lead fourth highest,
and a suit headed by no honour. From this combination, you
should lead a high card. Most players opt to lead the second
highest card.

So, from the following holdings, the underlined card would
be correct:

(a) 9*7*432,   (b) 8*6*53,   (c) 9*8*765,   (d) 9*7*5432

Once partner works out that your lead cannot be a fourth highest card, he should deduce that you hold length in the suit, but no honour at the head of it. As a result, on gaining the lead, partner may switch to a different suit, rather than returning yours.

These three different types of lead should make you analyze your partner's led card as follows:

Honour led = Top of a sequence.
Little card led = 4th highest from a suit headed by an honour.
High intermediate led = suit headed by no honour card.

There is really only one further basic principle to reinforce about defending NT contracts. That is partnership co-operation. Making tricks in NTs is simply about setting up your longest suit by pushing out your opponents' high cards until your little cards have become winners. To achieve this successfully as defenders, it is nearly always right to keep attacking the same suit. If you switch from suit to suit, trying to grab the occasional trick, you will find declarer triumphant with monotonous regularity. If you plough on with your own longest suit at every opportunity, you will find that, much more often, yours will be the side chalking up the plus score at the end of the hand.

This example is typical of a successful NT defence:

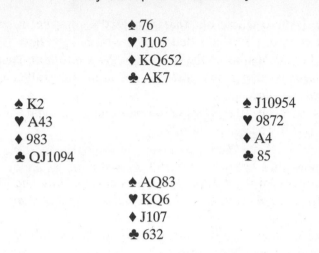

♠ 76
♥ J105
♦ KQ652
♣ AK7

♠ K2
♥ A43
♦ 983
♣ QJ1094

♠ J10954
♥ 9872
♦ A4
♣ 85

♠ AQ83
♥ KQ6
♦ J107
♣ 632

South plays in 3NT and you, as West, lead Q♣. Declarer wins the trick in dummy with A♣, and plays diamonds until East wins with his A♦, probably on the second round.

What should East return now? He can see K♣ still guarding the suit in dummy, and he does have an attractive sequence in spades. Should he switch to J♠? Definitely not.

There are two good reasons for this. Firstly, you have led a club, presumably because you hold a long suit, and have at least one entry in another suit with which to regain the lead (if you had held a really weak hand, you would not have led your longest suit). Secondly, East has no other means of regaining the lead now that he has won the trick with A♦, so even if a spade switch worked brilliantly, he could not get back on lead to enjoy the long suit. East must return his 8♣, and this will defeat the contract.

Whatever South plays, you just cover forcing out K♣. When you gain the lead with A♥, or even K♠, you will be able to cash your three club winners, defeating the contract.

Generally then, when defending a NT contract:

You should return partner's led suit when you gain the lead, unless he has led a high card from a poor holding, or you have a very good alternative suit of your own <u>combined with outside entries to regain the lead</u>.

Above all, keep asking yourself questions about how the bidding ran, and what this means about the other hands at the table. Count the points that declarer shows up with as he plays his own cards. You may gain a vital insight into the lie of certain cards. If a declarer has opened 1NT and shows up with 12pts, then he cannot also hold that missing King you were worrying about. That would give him too many points. Your partner must have it and, all of a sudden, you may be able to see the killing defence. The satisfaction when this moment arrives and your strategy works is well worth the hard work you've put into it.

It's intoxicating…

14

PARTNERSHIP DISCUSSIONS

You sit down with a new partner, perhaps a whole table of strangers. What should you do? If you're playing for money, try not to look nervous. It's extraordinary how money seems to leave the purses of the nervous. If it's a social game, be sociable.

Now, what about the bridge?

However well you think your partner plays, and especially if you don't know, I recommend adoption of the following technique:

(Firmly, but with a smile)

YOU: "I'm sure you play far better than me, so would you mind if we played:

Weak No-Trump (12–14pts)

Stayman, opposite 1NT & 2NT (Modified Baron opposite 2NT?)

Take-Out Doubles over opposition pre-empts

Blackwood, and **Cue-bidding** (deny any knowledge of Gerber)

Unusual NT Overcalls

Asptro?" (if partner isn't sure, don't bother)

Discuss, momentarily, **signals** and **discards** in defence – most people throw high cards in suits they want you to lead, and low ones in suits they don't want you to lead. (Incidentally, I recommend that <u>you</u> don't bother with the first bit, and just *throw away what you don't want*.) A sound maxim, if ever I heard one...

If you know that you really are better than your partner, then try to do whatever he would like. If your partner is relaxed, he will play far better than if you try to educate him at the table.

Finally, once the play has started, say only two things:

"Well played, partner" or, frankly, more lightly, "Bad luck, partner". Then recommend this book...

ABBREVIATIONS

C D H S	Representing the suits in the bidding, and final contract.
NT	No-Trumps.
Dbl	Double.
Rdl	Redouble.
♣ ♦ ♥ ♠	Representing the suits in cards played.
RHO	Right hand opponent.
LHO	Left hand opponent.
HCP	High Card Points.
4SF	Fourth Suit Forcing. (Ref: page 57.)
DGR	Delayed Game Raise. (Ref: page 31.)
GSF	Grand Slam Force. (Ref: page 138.)
x	A small card, not an honour.
AKQJ	Representing honour cards.
5-4-3-1	Representing the shape of the hand, with suits in no particular order.

DEFINITIONS

Balanced   distribution of the cards in your hand; no more than 8 cards between your two longest suits. (Ref: page 9.)

Balancing   making a protective bid. (Ref: page 159.)

Conventional Bid   a cipher bid, containing agreed information, which has no connection to the suit bid (i.e. Stayman; Blackwood).

Cue-bid
– Immediate   ref: page 118.
– Slam-investigating   ref: page 140.
– Unassuming   ref: page 112.

Defensive trick(s)   trick(s) likely to make whilst defending opponents' contract.

Distributional   distribution of the cards in your hand. Unbalanced. At least 9 cards between your two longest suit. (Ref: page 14.)

Duplicate Pairs   a form of competitive bridge in which all competitors play the same hands over the course of a session and their results are directly compared to find the winner.

"First and second in hand" the dealer, and the second person who has an opportunity to bid.

Fit length in the same suit, held between partners. You would be said to "have a fit with partner" if you held a minimum of 8 cards between your two hands.

Forcing for 1 round partner MUST bid at least once more.

Forcing to Game the bidding must continue until Game is reached.

Fourth Suit Forcing ref: page 57.

Game-going hand a hand on which you believe Game should now be bid on the basis of your partner's bidding to date.

Laydown description of a contract in which all the tricks are obviously there. Sometimes, in play, the hand is laid down on the table for all four players to see.

Misfit a deal when your side does not hold more than seven cards between you in any of the suits.

Opener the first player to make a positive bid, <u>not</u> No-bid.

Playing Trick(s) card or cards, likely to make "in the play". (Ref: page 82.)

Reverse ref: page 42.

Ruff trump.

Ruffing Value a shortage in a suit, usually in dummy, which declarer can use to trump (ruff) his losers.

Self-supporting suit a suit requiring no cards in support from partner to make it an acceptable trump suit.

Sign-off a bid intended to conclude the auction for your side (e.g. Weak Take-Out. Ref: page 18.)

Slim contract contract bid (and likely to make) with fewer points than one would normally expect to be required.

Solid suit   suit headed by an unbroken sequence of top honours.

Stopper; stop   – usually in NTs; a card (or cards) which can <u>stop</u> opponents from running off a long suit against you.

Throw-in   a deal when all four players pass, and the cards are literally, thrown in, to be dealt again.

Trial Bid   ref: page 46.

Underbid   a bid which deliberately indicates a holding/point count less good than that which you actually hold.

Undertrick(s)   trick(s) by which you have failed to make your contract.

Unguarded suit   a suit containing no high cards/stoppers.

Weak Take-Out   ref: page 18.